Video

The .... na
of c .... ar-
kete .... ust
abo .... ial
skill .... ers
war

I .... ir-
ing .... eir
effc

•
•
•
•
•

E .... es-
tio .... eed
to

Pe .... of
Go .... try,
its .... oks
and

Mi .... len,
wh .... na-
lyst .... ion,
also due in 2016 from Routledge.

"The divide between videogame marketing and videogame development has stood cavernous. In this text, Zackariasson and Dymek simultaneously forge new connections between these worlds and bridge gaps between games as art and games as business. In doing so, the book contributes significantly to our understanding of games and videogames as cultural products rather than simply 'toys' or software sold for entertainment. Videogames are serious business."

Casey O'Donnell, *Associate Professor in the Department of Media and Information, Michigan State University, USA*

Video Game Marketing
A student textbook

Peter Zackariasson and Mikolaj Dymek

Routledge
Taylor & Francis Group

LONDON AND NEW YORK

First published 2017
by Routledge
2 Park Square, Milton Park, Abingdon, Oxon OX14 4RN

And by Routledge
711 Third Avenue, New York, NY 10017

Routledge is an imprint of the Taylor & Francis Group, an informa business

© 2017 Peter Zackariasson and Mikolaj Dymek

British Library Cataloguing in Publication Data
A catalogue record for this book is available from the British Library

Library of Congress Cataloging in Publication Data
Names: Zackariasson, Peter, 1972- author. | Dymek, Mikolaj, author.
Title: Video game marketing : a student textbook / Peter Zackariasson and Mikolaj Dymek.
Description: Abingdon, Oxon ; New York, NY : Routledge, 2017. | Includes bibliographical references and index.
Identifiers: LCCN 2016014153 | ISBN 9781138812260 (hardback) | ISBN 9781138812277 (pbk.) | ISBN 9781315748900 (ebook)
Subjects: LCSH: Video games industry. | Video games—Marketing.
Classification: LCC HD9993.E452 Z33 2017 | DDC 794.8068/8—dc23
LC record available at https://lccn.loc.gov/2016014153

ISBN: 978-1-138-81226-0 (hbk)
ISBN: 978-1-138-81227-7 (pbk)
ISBN: 978-1-315-74890-0 (ebk)

Typeset in Bembo
by Apex CoVantage, LLC

Contents

Figures

Introduction

This is a book about marketing, more specifically about marketing and video games. In a relatively short time period we have seen video games flood a great many areas of life. There is no longer any doubt that this medium is having a huge impact on our way of life. This has been the case since the 1960s, when video games first were starting to entertain us. This will also be the case in the future – no doubt! The possibilities open to this medium are endless, and we have as yet explored only a fraction of them. We believe that video games are an extremely powerful medium that can engage and mesmerize us, entertain and educate us. They can do all of these things – if we put our minds to releasing their potential. With this book we hope to make a humble contribution to the further exploration and development of video games. This is a journey that will benefit from many different kinds of knowledge – not the least marketing.

This book is about using marketing knowledge as a tool in the development of video games so that the games achieve their goals: having wide impact, creating a groundbreaking genre or challenging the concept of games themselves – or any other goal that you as a developer set for yourself. We believe that applying marketing to game development makes it possible to conceptualize the market for a game: how you relate to video games as a developer and to the consumers who are going to play your game, as well as the structure in which your games are supposed to sell and have an impact on the industry, the press or society. Marketing is for us a way of thinking about and a tool for the development of experiences for consumers. It structures how you relate to all aspects of developing and communicating whatever games you develop.

This book, to be even more specific, is for those of you who want to build a game company – not just games. From our experiences as researchers and lecturers we know that there is a huge number of talented people out there, people who are passionate about games but who also have the technical skills required to build great games: skills in programming, graphics, design, sound, music and more. Unfortunately we have also seen many of these talented people embark on development projects full of enthusiasm for making "the best game ever!", only to see their games drown in the flood of the thousands of game releases each year. Or they may find out after launch that the people who actually shared their vision for "the best game ever" constituted only a handful of devoted hard-core gamers. We believe that using marketing skills to improve both game development and market communication provides knowledge that is pivotal in developing games that have a major impact. Marketing can thus present useful tools to propel passionate and skillful people in building game companies that develop games that make a difference.

Before we set off into the land of marketing, it is valuable to describe how we, as authors of this book, view games, the industry and marketing. There are many viewpoints on each of those topics. And there should be! That is partly what makes discussing video games interesting. But, in order for you to understand the arguments we make here, it is valuable for us to lay out our starting points and assumptions.

Our starting point as gamers

Both of us have long and passionate relationships with video games. Although neither of us has actually participated in the development of games, we have both played games and researched the game industry from early 2000 onwards. We would guess that our exposure to games, growing up in middle-class European families, looks much like any textbook description found on the shelves of a bookstore. Just like anyone else born in the 1970s we were among the first generation to define ourselves as gamers – Generation G – whereas all the generations that have grown up after us have incorporated games more and more into their daily media consumption. And, although our living arrangements nowadays include more responsibility, we, Generation G, are still playing video games.

Our first exposure to video games came in the early 1980s. At this point games were part of weekend hangouts in gaming parlours, arcade halls, amusement parks or shopping malls. Sometimes it took some real convincing before parents would let their kids go to what were in their eyes dodgy places. Parents seemed to be convinced that hanging out with friends and spending coins for the suspect purpose of looking at a screen could lead to no good. But in the early 1980s technological development opened up for a new kind of interaction with games, through the gaming console and personal computer. There was something magical about that piece of technology sitting there – in the living room. Peter was (to his utter anguish) not among the first ones who got one of these computers, but a friend of his was. We kids in school used to visit the friend's house during lunch breaks, well – most breaks, actually. And the only reason was that his father had bought the hottest new gadget of that time, a Commodore Vic 20. This was a very crude computer by today's standards, but those black blocks on the screen were enough for us kids to imagine ourselves being heroes or villains – chasing other black blocks that of course were dragons or monsters. It was a world of endless magic!

We played the few games available for that computer every way we could think of, every time waiting in suspense while the cassette player loaded the game. We tried to find the games' weaknesses, and indeed there were many, besides the bad graphics. We even made attempts to change the code of the software to beat the game – endless lives and what have you. Most of the time the only result was that the game would not even run after we had made what we thought were obvious improvements to the code. The point is that interacting with those early games was enough to evoke our interest in both video games and what they could do as a new medium for interaction – and to make us realize that neither of us would ever be able to code a game ourselves.

As we grew up, we got our own computers: consoles, handhelds, PCs, laptops and so on, not to mention the incredible Commodore Vic 128, that, sadly, Mikolaj completely missed out on. We also engaged in all sorts of games, for pleasure and for passing time. An interest in this medium would eventually lead us into studying game developers and the industry during our doctoral studies – one in business administration and the other in industrial economy.

Peter studied the Swedish developer Massive Entertainment and the Norwegian developer Funcom. He also devoted a great many hours to Funcom's online game Anarchy Online – of course, all in the name of science. It is called participant observations. In 2004, just like many others, he moved his gaming devotion to World of Warcraft – one of the most successful games in its genre, released in Europe by Blizzard Entertainment in 2005.

Mikolaj came to study the international video game industry and the start of a discipline to understand games – ludology. Through his work he has mapped out the structure of the industry, meeting both representatives from the industry and its consumers, tracking the formation of the industry from the small studio staff talking to a handful of developers to the major crazy at events that attract thousands and thousands of participants.

Our gaming experience follows that of Generation G. Our gaming is limited mostly to casual games, such as Candy Crush Saga, Plants vs. Zombies or some other game that you can play on your phone – in boring meetings, once you have gotten tired of writing books, or just while waiting for a bus. Like many others who started playing games in the 1980s, we still play. For us, this again leads to the future of video games. This medium has to grow with the audience. We have seen what it can do – where do we take it from here?

The games industry

One might say that the video game industry started in the 1960s in the basement of a Massachusetts Institute of Technology building, where students developed a "hack" for the PDP computer that recently had been purchased by the university. This resulted in Spacewar!, a game about two spaceships orbiting a moon. One could also say that the foundation for this industry was laid a decade earlier at Brookhaven National Laboratory with the game Tennis for Two. Or one could say that the industry took off a decade later with the introduction of the arcade video game Pong, developed by Atari. As a matter of fact, the precise time this industry was started, or took off, is a matter that is outside the scope of this book. The observations made here instead deal with our understanding of where this industry has ended up today.

By a popular comparison, it is claimed that revenues from video games passed revenues from the Hollywood box office around 2004. Financial size is indeed a compelling way to compare the two industries, but no matter how you slice the cake – economics, technical growth or cultural impact – the affect this industry is having on our society is major. The statistics from industry groups clearly show the spread of video games as part of popular culture. The importance of this is that today we have a population that plays, thinks and dreams about video games.

The industry has, for most of its history, managed to encapsulate this passion about games – developing games that are big sellers and those that challenge the medium. Although there are possibilities for improvements, games have come a long way in building a solid place in people's daily media consumption. We believe that in the future games will tell stories different from those they tell today, stories as diverse as those in movies and literature, that future games will offer different platforms for interaction and different outcomes from this interaction. Getting there will be the job for the next generation of developers.

The traditional setup of the industry is similar to that of other publishing industries, consisting of a value chain where each function is divided into different companies. A value chain is a description of the actors that are involved in creating value for a specific industry. Although this slowly is being diffused, much of the power of the industry still is dependent on the division: developer, publisher, distributor, retailer, customer and consumer.

Parts of the industry are still dependent on this value chain, but much of this is changing – mainly because of technical possibilities that allow us to circumvent traditional business relations. There are, for example, ample possibilities for self-publishing a game you have developed yourself. Many times this means greater freedom for the developer, but it also means that much of what was handled by publishers now has to be handled by the developer. More freedom thus means more responsibility; it also means that more knowledge has to reside within the developing company.

Although there are possibilities for shortening the value chain, there are actors who cannot be ignored. This leads us back to marketing. We believe that building a game company is much more than having a great idea for a game. Although there has to be an idea for a game, how you package and communicate that idea is equally important. If you have the possibility to work with a publisher, they will help you with some of these aspects – that is a benefit of

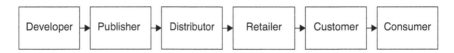

Figure 0.1 Traditional value chain in the video game industry

Source: Zackariasson and Wilson, 2012, p. 3

working with publishers. But, as a developer it is, at the end of the day, you who has to build a strong company that is able to churn out games that attract and fascinate gamers. Through applying a marketing perspective to your game company, you can start putting together great ideas for games with great market possibilities. This is what will put your company in the best position to grow.

What is marketing?

Because this is a book about marketing and video games, there are some things we do need to define at the outset. One of the major questions is: what is marketing? In laymen's terms, you might say that marketing is the knowledge of how to create value for other people – or, to be more specific, how to make gamers interested in your games. On the surface this seems an easy enough deal, right? If that is all marketing is, then why are there university programs and courses? Well, it turns out that once we take on board this obvious definition, there is more to it – much more. Marketing is both a practice and a philosophy, both a toolbox of activities and a viewpoint on how to analyze and understand what is happening around us.

A common misconception of marketing is that it deals with advertising exclusively, as if marketing were something that you bring along late in the process – once the product is done, now let's market this! You might have heard that yourself. Sadly, this is how marketing is often practiced, as if it were a sales function with no input into corporate strategy or product development. When talking to many game developers about marketing, this is what we often hear, as if marketing were what you do to get people interested in a product you already have, the magic stardust sprinkled on a game in order to attract the attention of gamers. In our view this is an all too narrow view of marketing. It keeps marketing practices from having the biggest impact they can have and divides marketing into bits of knowledge. But, yes, advertising is part of marketing, a part that is successful only to close the marketing communication. In order for advertising to work, it has to be implemented in relation to a strategic marketing approach.

The American Marketing Association, the organization that has taken upon itself to standardize concepts and understanding of different marketing concepts, defines marketing this way: "Marketing is the activity, set of institutions, and processes for creating, communicating, delivering, and exchanging offerings that have value for customers, clients, partners, and society at large." In this definition marketing is all about creating value. We also lean toward this definition. But when it comes to video games there is more to it than that. As part of the culture industries, video games have other dimensions that have to be taken into account, aspects that all cultural expressions share: symbolical value, aesthetic value and so on.

Marketing for cultural industries is thus different from marketing for industries that produce cars, mobiles or toilet papers. When applying marketing tools and marketing philosophies, it is important to understand the difference. Video games and other cultural offerings contain more symbolical messaging than do other products. This means that what is communicated through these products is closer to the arts, of comments on different aspects on society. Other products have less messaging value, although most consumption that we engage in has more to do with consuming symbols and concepts than with meeting actual needs.

Before we end this short introduction to marketing, it is important that we reflect on the models and theories you will come across on different aspects of marketing and how these can be used. The social sciences rarely deal with something we call "facts". Theories and models in social sciences are to a large degree simplifications of phenomena we try to understand. There is thus no direct correlation between theory and phenomenon. This leaves us with two conclusions for now. The theories and models presented here can be used in two ways. First, they are tools to think with. They have the ability to structure how you relate to markets, products, consumers or other aspects in marketing. There is a saying that the best theory is a useful theory. The second conclusion is that theories help you to see things that you normally would not. This has to do with perspectives and what all of us assume about what we encounter on a daily basis. Any setting, any process, any object can be understood from a number of different viewpoints. The more perspectives you have the capability to incorporate, the more reflexive you can be in your approach. Marketing is thus one of many ways to understand game development.

About this book

This book is written for those of you who are developing video games and those of you who are studying in order to pursue a career developing video games. It is not a traditional book on game development in the sense that you will learn all the tricks of the trade in making games. We believe that the books available today fill that purpose quite well, and we do not have the ability to bring additional knowledge to that discussion. But, through our knowledge of marketing and the video game industry we do offer a way to frame your game development in a way that marketing can help you create and organize your game development company, then build and communicate your games. Although there are many university programs for learning the craft of developing video games, very few of these teach marketing – or any other business-related knowledge (to our knowledge). Considering the large number of persons starting their own game development studios after graduation, this is quite surprising. Running a business developing, communicating and selling video games requires additional knowledge beyond the craft of making these games. This book is thus for you who want to create an excellent game company, not only excellent games.

The book consists of twelve chapters, divided into three different parts. These parts are thematically framed in order to communicate aspects of marketing that relate both to a certain area and to a certain way to understand marketing. As we argued earlier, marketing is not one single perspective. Marketing can be both a philosophy and a set of tools that help you to structure game development or communication with gamers. Therefore, we believe that it is vital that all of these aspects have a presence in this book. In traditional marketing education students are taken on a journey from practical tools toward more philosophical and critical ideas about marketing. The three parts of each chapter should therefore be understood as three ways to explore marketing in the video game industry. They can all strengthen game development, either as single tools or as ways of thinking about markets.

The first part explores marketing as a *practical tool* that can help you strategically build a company and the value the company aims at offering. This means that marketing now is a toolbox, full of different tools that can be applied to different aspects of game development and game company challenges. As tools they all play important roles if applied correctly to the right problem. These two aspects – correct use of the tools for appropriate problems – increase the possibility of beneficial outcomes for developers who use marketing tools. It is also equally important to point out that the tools presented here are theories of social sciences. This means that the tools have been constructed to describe a generalized field of marketing, all situations being equal – thus handled equally. We know that this is not the case; there are always differences. Thus we are urging you to consider a *critical application* of these tools. Use them as tools for structuring how you understand aspects in games development. Keep in mind that things that do not easily fall into the model can be as important as, if not more important, than those that work easily with it. The aim is thus not to find that these tools can be applied to your company; they can all be applied to different companies and different processes. The question you should ask yourself is how these tools will help your company to improve.

There are six chapters on different marketing tools in the first part. The aspects of building a game development company and developing video games that they highlight are the ones we think are most important for start-ups. As your organization grows and your game production gets more elaborate, you will use other aspects of marketing. (1) 'The market for video games' positions game development in relation to the persons who are playing the game. In marketing we call these consumers and customers, and in the video game industry they are mostly referred to as gamers. No matter how we define these persons, they are the most important aspect of game development; thus we also start here. (2) 'Marketing strategy and the marketing mix' deals with some fundamental aspects of setting up your game development company. Knowing what you do and for whom will enable you to construct a clear idea for the persons working in your company and will also make it easier to develop games and communicate with consumers in a way that is in line with this strategy. (3) 'Video games as products or services' explore what it is you are offering through video games. Traditionally marketing has dealt with products; this is also how the video game industry has understood games. But the changes that have occurred within the strong presence of digital communication and social media strongly suggest that games are best understood as services. (4) 'Brands and video games' deals with the importance of associations. In marketing this is mostly dealt with through strategic application of brands. These are both visual and conceptual tools to strengthen messaging value of games. (5) 'Market communication of video games' uses the knowledge that has been communicated throughout previous chapters and explores how this can be used in order to create successful communication with consumers. (6) 'Market research for games development' presents a structural way game developers can gather and use information about market and consumer.

The second part of this book *challenges* marketing from a philosophical viewpoint and ends with what we believe the future of video game development might be. Much of the knowledge in this part also, in what might seem as a counter-productive move, turns against what has been communicated in the first part. The premise of the first part was that marketing can be equated with a natural science and that there are clear laws and rules that govern behaviour in a market. Thus, the models we apply have a relation to a market "out there". As much as this seems appealing, it is not the case. One market, as much as any social setting, rarely takes the same shape as any other market. Any attempt to generalize about how markets work will fail miserably. But tools that have the possibility to help you find your way in games development, as presented in the first part, are vital in order to make sense of any market and to operate in that market.

Further, a philosophical standpoint has the ability to challenge what is taken for granted in games development in order to improve that same market. As the popular metaphor of the jazz player implies, it is hard to improvise and challenge conventional music if you first do not learn musical scales. The knowledge that is communicated throughout this part can thus help you improve your relationship with marketing knowledge. The point here is that no knowledge should be approached uncritically. Challenge what is communicated to you; challenge all knowledge with an educated mind!

This is explored throughout three chapters. (1) 'Postmodern marketing' is a result of the postmodern turn in the 1960s and 1970s. Postmodernity refuses grand explanations and structures; this in turn makes it possible to explore alternative ways to build a relationship between game and gamer. (2) 'Marketing as practice' builds on a practice turn that has had an impact on marketing since the turn of the century. Focusing on what people actually do when they play games enables us to strengthen practices for our games. (3) 'The future of game development' will not have the same philosophical focus as such, but in this chapter we offer what we believe is a possible and challenging way forward for the video game industry.

In the third and last part of the book we *explore* different promotional approaches that we believe have had an important impact on game development and that can continue to do so. These are examples of how marketing can be very creatively applied to how games are communicated to consumers. The examples brought forward here are both informative and inspirational. Marketing is but a tool, a way of thinking, but how it is applied is completely up to you. We hope that you do see the value in building on the tools presented in part one, in challenging these as presented in part two and in getting creative and finding new and intriguing ways, as suggested in part three.

The chapters included in this part offer three examples. (1) 'Advergames and in-game advertising' are one form of promotion. Games themselves have a high communication value that can be used for promoting other products, both as game in themselves but also through the inclusion of advertisements in the virtual worlds of existing games. (2) 'Gamification' seems to be among the latest application of game structures in non-gaming settings. Although these structure are not new to the industry, gamification offers an interesting way to gamify other consumer interactions. (3) The last example is that of 'Alternate Reality Games'. These are highly engaging promotional games that have been used to promote both cultural products, such as games, and other consumer products.

Part I
Tools

1 The market for video games

In this first chapter we turn our focus away from why we develop video games and ask instead for whom we develop video games. We argue that successful marketing means turning to consumers before even starting development. Successful video games, in terms of building a business, are not built for ourselves or our peers – they are built for a consumer audience that will gladly pay for them. This is the so-called marketing-focused process as opposed to a product-focused approach. First we start with the consumers and segment them into target groups. We continue by positioning our game title within this segmentation. We end this chapter by explaining how we can take into account the various types of buying behaviour by analyzing the buying-decision process that drives different behaviour.

Learning objectives

1 To understand the difference between a product-focused game development process and a marketing-focused game development process
2 To learn the basic processes of identifying the consumers of your game
3 To recognize the fundamental properties of consumer behaviour

Introduction

We believe that the most important person in the business of making video games is the consumer or gamer, as the consumer is usually referred to in the video game industry. No matter your dreams or aspirations, this is the person for whom you are developing games. This is the person who is willing to spend time and hard-earned money to buy your games. It makes sense to develop games with that specific person in mind, incorporating what this person will want to see in the game while it is planned. There are today processes in most game studios to deal with this aspect, including experience from developing other games and agile project models. In this chapter we have a look at how game development benefits from relating to consumers as future market possibilities. This includes generating knowledge about consumers, using this in the development of games and in the end communicating to these consumers.

Games for whom?

Video games are part of the cultural industry. They are cultural products and something that many of us interact with on a daily basis. The result of this categorization is that both production and consumption of games are assumed to be different from those for other products. That is, games are compared with music, movies and novels – instead of toothpaste, bikes or computers. With the latter products there is a clear relation between developers and consumers. These also assume development of goods to satisfy different needs and wants (more about this later). The relationship to cultural products is a bit more complicated, as the motivation to both produce and consume culture is different from using, let's say, toothpaste. What all cultural products have in common is that they inhabit symbolical value about society – love, friendship, conflict, money or other things that mean much to us in our societies.

When looking at the cultural industries as a whole, there are three different potential consumers for what is developed: (1) oneself, (2) peers, (3) consumers (see figure 1.1). It also appears that it does not matter very much what type of culture we are talking about. There are today both cultural and technical possibilities to engage with a lot of cultural productions – for different reasons. Throughout your education or working experience, we expect that you also have had the same experience. There are persons who develop games for themselves. The person developing the game is then also the main audience, and the reward of viewing and interacting with the game is the sole purpose of development. Games are here seen as constructed to materialize an emotion,

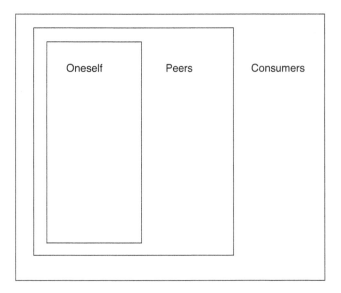

Figure 1.1 Different consumers for cultural products

Source: Hirschman, 1983, p. 49

viewpoint – or whatever one wants to express with the game. This can be compared with the saying "art for art's sake", that is, art has no meaning but itself. It is important that the development process starts with the individual and end with the individual. There are also games that are produced for a smaller number of persons, mainly colleagues or other persons in the games industry. The reason for developing this game is to generate credit from persons within the industry and to show off the capability of the person(s) who has made the game. We all know the importance of portfolios for future projects or future employments, so it makes sense to communicate within the industry, to one's peers and colleagues, in order to make a name for oneself.

Now, we can agree that both of these reasons for making games are in themselves legitimate and respectable reasons for making games. We all appreciate video games as a medium for visualizing and communicating cultural value, and entertainment. But when it comes to building a business for video games, we believe that the focus needs to shift from oneself and one's peers to consumers. As described in the model, this is the third possible audience for games. This means moving from one's own evaluation on game quality, moving away from peers and colleagues and moving into a consideration of what consumers might enjoy and prefer. We realize that this sounds suspicious and many times it is hard to do in practice. But the possibility to generate sales and a sustainable game development business increases if you know who you are developing games for, why these consumers should be interested in your game and how you best communicate with these consumers.

"If we build it, they will come"

There are, in general, two different processes that function as rationales for any development project: a *product-focused process* and a *marketing-focused process*. This is the case for both the video game industry and for other industries. In these two processes a product is developed either looking internally (in the company to see what could successfully be produced) or externally (to determine what consumers are looking for). A *product-focused process* starts with the skills and manufacturing possibilities that exist in the company. This can be viewed as a traditional engineering starting point. For example a technical idea is developed as an innovation. The rationale is that the development is driven by the competence in the company and what possibilities these have for developing the idea. Once the development is done, it is a matter of selling – hard selling! – of finding the customers who are willing to buy what has been developed. We call this perspective "if we build it, they will come."

This process is quite common among a large number of industries, not least in the video game industry. There is a belief that if a game is just good enough according to the developers themselves, the customers will buy the game. Unfortunately, this process has a risk of failure as the gap between the game and the expectations from consumers can be quite wide, resulting in the game drowning in the flood of games published each month and subsequently generating low sales. There are good things to say about this approach, for example the possibility to innovate and push technological boundaries without pressure for commercial use or the fun of making a game for oneself and not giving a toss about what anyone else thinks. Quite a few products that we today have on the market have come about this way, and if there are possibilities to pursue this focus it can result in good products – games and game technology. Our experience, however, is that many start-ups do not have the financial possibilities or the experience to commercialize ground-breaking innovations. The gap between the game and market expectations can become too wide and a hard sell of the game becomes problematic as consumers try to understand what the game is all about.

Some of you might object at this point: "What about Mojang?" (or any other game whose developer obviously did not give a toss about the consumer). Its producers managed to develop a game out of pure belief and hit the big jackpot. And yes, there are a few games that have followed this trajectory. These are brought forward as examples of people who got away with building something in their basement that they were convinced would be a great game. We all love those stories! But, for the thousands of games that generate low sales following the same belief we would recommend a *marketing-focused process*.

A marketing-focused process

A marketing-focused process starts with the consumer. It starts with asking about the needs and wants of the consumer at whom you are aiming. In marketing it is argued that we all have a number of basic *needs* that can be sorted into five categories (see figure 1.2): physiological (food, water, sleep), safety (security of body, employment, resources), belonging (friendship, family, intimacy), esteem (self-esteem, confidence, respect) and self-actualization (morality, creativity, spontaneity). According to this model one cannot create needs; these are inherent in being human and fixed in time and space. But, as we are sure you suspect from your interaction with marketing this far, that is not the whole truth. As a conceptual framework for thinking about games and the need they fulfill, the model makes sense – food is more important than games. But, if we depend too much on models like this, we miss the facts that needs are culturally dependent: they vary according to where we live, how we are raised, who we are friends with and all other aspects of our lives. But just as our lives change, so do our needs.

One example that very well highlights this is the Tamagotchi. When Bandai developed the Tamagotchi in 1996 it did not create a need to care for electronic pets; it instead created an electronic device that would speak to the need for belonging and caring. Although the need for belonging can be satisfied in a number of different ways, this is where different *wants* come into play. It is possible to create a number of different wants in order to satisfy needs. The most obvious example is our physiological needs, for example thirst. This can be satisfied in many different ways, such as with water. But creating a beverage that the

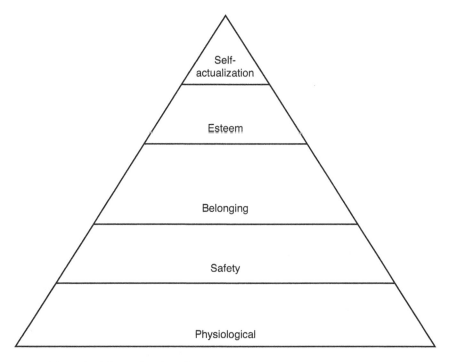

Figure 1.2 Maslow's hierarchy of needs

Source: Maslow, 1954, p. 80

customer wants each time he or she is thirsty is beneficial for a producer. Instead of thinking "I'm thirsty," one thinks, "I'm thirsty for a Coke," for example.

In a marketing-focused process, consumers' needs and wants are inputs to the development of a product. Using knowledge from consumer behaviour, from preferences in existing products, and from marketing research, it is possible to construct an understanding of what kind of games a customer would like to see. What are the patterns for games right now in a specific market? Are there any games on the market that seem to attract much attention? What are the behaviours of current gamers? These questions can generate a good picture of those a game is developed for. Of course, it is not possible to develop a game on the basis of this knowledge alone. The mission of the company or ambitions to drive new and innovative genres have to be taken into account. Consumer knowledge thus has to be related to knowledge and ambitions inside the company – both the developer's and the publisher's.

The reason we argue for a marketing approach when developing video games is that both the development process and marketing communication will thus have clear aims. They support each other as the company develops games that consumers are more likely to buy.

Consumer–customer

We hope that by now it is quite clear that knowing for whom you are developing games and how you communicate with these persons is pivotal. We have been talking exclusively about the consumer, but there are in fact a number of different persons involved in buying games. We primarily tend to think and talk about the person who is playing games, that is, the gamer. In marketing terminology this is the consumer – the person consuming a product or service. Although this person is the focus, as it should be, there are reasons to expand our view and include other roles to which we have to relate when developing video games. The term "customer" is many times used interchangeably with "consumer". Although they can refer to the same person, the meaning is slightly different. Whereas the consumer consumes, the customer is entering into an exchange relationship for games; that is, a customer buys games. As many of us today are buying games online, we are the customers of publishers, but we are also consumers as we are playing the games. Of course, there are cases when games are purchased to be given as presents and parents buy games for kids. So, in the end, who are you to communicate with when developing games?

Segmentation

In order to develop a game aimed for a specific consumer or customer, we do of course want to know as much as possible about that person or persons. This is where the process of *segmentation* starts, in order to construct knowledge about consumer behaviour – what games are preferred and how that person buys and plays games. A market segment is a group of consumers who respond in a similar way to a given set of marketing efforts. Traditionally the segments that have dominated the game industry have been hard-core and casual gamers, or people organized by dimensions such as gender or age. Although this rubric categorizes how the person plays games (or so we think) and how engaged that person is, it still remains a rather crude road map for making games.

In marketing segmentation we use a number of different dimensions in order to construct different segments of consumers. These dimensions are cultural, social, personal and psychological (see figure 1.3). The cultural dimensions are the most basic determinant of a person's wants and behaviour. We all grow up in a specific culture that we share with those around us. We are thus socialized into a setting when we grow up and later also when we meet friends and colleagues. But we can also think of culture as consisting of smaller groups, often referred to as subcultures. These comprise a number of persons who share values and interest that are not part of mainstream culture.

The social dimension concerns how we relate to other persons. We humans are social beings, that is, we like to spend time with other humans. And when doing so we affect others, just as they have an effect on us. Just think about whom you consult when buying a video game or any other product for that matter. It could be your friend, your colleagues or social media. In that way word of mouth is one of the most powerful influences on people buying video games. Using it as a tool

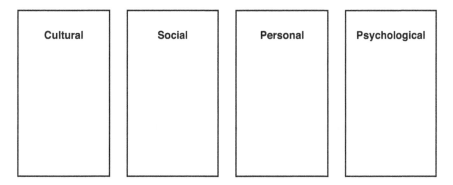

Figure 1.3 Factors influencing consumer behaviour

Source: Kotler et al., 2008, p. 240

is sometimes also referred to as buzz marketing. The point is here to identify an opinion leader in a social setting, a person who has high social capital and is trusted by many, and have that person create a buzz for a specific product.

The personal dimension is related to the situation of a particular person. It includes how old the person is and in what phase of life. What occupation does the consumer have, and what does his or her economic situation look like? On the personal aspect it is also possible to draw out what kind of personality and lifestyle the person has. Independent of the fact that we indeed are social beings, we also have individual personalities that affect how we relate to the world. This affects how we, as consumers, buy and play games. Many of these factors have an impact on this. You may be a poor student with ample time but little money or a person with a well-paid job but little time to play. The concept of lifestyle is also worth exploring a bit, being something of a favourite concept in many marketing settings. Included in lifestyle are a number of different traits. It is thought persons share attitudes and beliefs within that lifestyle. For example we can assume that Live Action Role Play is a lifestyle. This builds on shared beliefs about certain behaviours and about relations to popular culture and to products that support this lifestyle. So as a LARPer you can recognize others within that same lifestyle through items and behaviour. Other examples include metal-heads, skaters and hipsters.

The last dimension is the psychological. This is where things can be a bit tricky as we now are wandering into the world of psychology. Now we are interested in what motivates an individual to buy games, and play games. What are that person's beliefs about games and society in general? We are also interested in a person's beliefs and attitudes. The point is that knowing these aspects of consumers is extremely beneficial for any developer, but extracting this data is both costly and sometimes quite questionable in terms of ethics and reliability. Still, the more we know about the persons we want to buy our games, the better off we are.

Using these dimensions there are a number of different ways to move forward. Either we can start with existing markets for games that already have been released, or we can start looking at gamers in general and categorize these according to a selection of the dimensions we have discussed. The benefit of working with a database of existing consumers is that much information on the personal dimension should also be available, such as age, occupation, purchase history and so on. This gives us a basis for understanding different segments that are already playing our games. If we are looking at game consumers in general, not having a database of gamers available, it is a matter of finding different types of consumers and what sets them apart from one another.

The end result from segmenting consumers should be a number of different categories of gamers – persons who share distinctive traits related to how they buy games, how they play games, why they play and other relevant dimensions. With this information at hand it is possible to move to the next phase – choosing one segment to focus on when developing a game.

Positioning

There are only a few products that have the capability to attract a large number of different segments. These *undifferentiated* products are mostly things that we all need at one point or another, such as milk. We know milk use is culturally dependent, so in other countries than Sweden there might be other goods that have the same position. But in Sweden we like our milk! The point is that when developing a game you should have one segment of consumers in mind. Developing a game for everyone is close to impossible!

Positioning is a process by which a developer constructs a game that has a clear, distinctive and desirable place within the target segment. As you are probably not the only developer with one specific segment of consumer in mind, there is a need to decide what segment you are developing your game for and how this game is different than other games on the market or in development if you have that information. A desired position is then the result of knowing all potential consumers of games, having divided them into different segments, depending on their cultural, social, personal and psychological profiles.

Types of buying-decision behaviour

We all buy games in different ways. That is, we are separated by the decisions we make and how we make them. As a developer you need to know this. When a consumer is engaged in buying any product, his or her behaviour varies depending on how involved the consumer is and how the consumer perceives differences between brands. As for games, we know that most consumers tend to be very much involved in the product, and they also have a lot of knowledge about the brands they are buying and the genre. In marketing we differentiate among four different kinds of buying behaviour: complex, dissonance-reducing, habitual and variety-seeking.

A complex buying behaviour occurs when there is a high involvement and significant perceived differences among brands. This means that the consumer perceives the importance of making the right decision. Not just any game will do here, because of the perceived differences among brands. In high-involvement buying behaviour consumers engage with searching for information about different products. As these games matter to them, they are much more likely to participate in communities to exchange information, look up facts about developers or engage with other consumers about their attitudes and opinions.

Dissonance-reducing buying behaviour has the same involvement as complex buying behaviour, but refers to situations in which the difference between different brands is not as clear and the difference between two games is not as evident. But, as the consumer is highly involved in the decision, there is also the feeling of "having to make the right decisions" and the angst of making the wrong one – "what if I buy the wrong game?" This situation is not ideal for the developer or for consumers and points up the importance of positioning games so that what they offer is differentiated from the attributes of other games.

Variety-seeking buying behaviour has a low involvement from the consumer and the differences between brands are perceived as significant. As with any other buying behaviours, these two dimensions define how a consumer acts. In this situation it could be the fact that the consumer is dealing with a well-known brand. A new game by a well-known developer attracts more attention. Buying that game thus has more to do with that developer than with the game itself.

Habitual buying behaviour also has low consumer involvement, but in this case the difference between the different brands is considered unimportant. Again, this is where we can bring back the milk example (yes, we know – it's a cultural thing). There are things that we buy out of habit, and what brand we buy does not make that much difference, we think. You might also want to think about the bored gamer here, a person who wants a new game, browses Steam, the Android Market or the App Store for any game that will do.

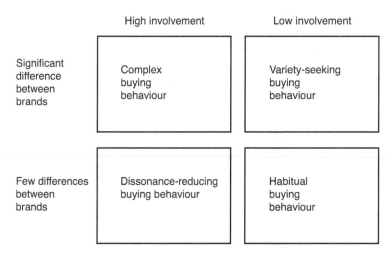

Figure 1.4 Four types of buying behaviour

Source: Assael, 1988, p. 67

When designing your games and planning its marketing, you need to consider what type of genre it represents and what kind of consumer involvement it evokes and also the positioning of your titles in relation to other similar titles – will it stand out in the crowd, or is the strategy to be similar?

Buying-decision process

Now that we have looked at the different dimensions that explain how we can understand a consumer and the different types of buying behaviour, we are ready to look at how consumers make buying decisions. The actual purchase of a game is part of a larger process, called the decision-making process. Knowing this process helps us to both provide appropriate information to consumers when they want it and increase potential interaction to facilitate a satisfactory purchase of a game. The point is that you as developer or publisher and marketer want to be involved in the whole process: need recognition, information search, evaluation of alternatives, purchase decision and post-purchase behaviour.

Although the process describes a movement from need recognition to post-purchase behaviour, there are differences depending on what type of purchase the consumer is engaged in. Habitual buying behaviours do not require either need recognition or information search – when there is a new Call of Duty out in the store, you buy one, for example. But, if you are spending your hard-earned

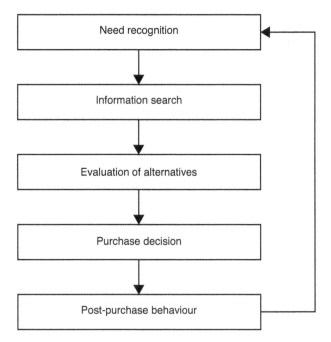

Figure 1.5 Buying-decision process

Source: Kotler et al., 2008, p. 265

money on a new strategy game, a genre you have little knowledge of, you are engaged in both information search and evaluation of alternatives. No matter the type of buying decision, we need to point out that successful developers have managed to insert themselves into the mind of consumers before this process starts. This means that they have reached something referred to as *top of mind*, brands that are already present when the consumer enters into a buying-decision process. This has the effect that the customer does not think, "I need a new graphics processor" but instead thinks, "I need a new NVIDIA graphics processor."

Need recognition is the starting point of most buying decisions. Here a consumer perceives a problem or need that needs attention. This recognition can come from *internal stimuli*: a consumer wants a new game because there are no fun games on the shelf at home anymore. But it can also be *external stimuli* that prompt this need recognition, such as a discussion with friends or being exposed to a promotion for a new game. In this stage it is important for us to understand the process of when a stimulus arises and why consumers decide to buy a game.

The second stage is information search. As mentioned, a consumer who is highly involved in the buying decision and who is making a complex decision is much likelier to engage in searching for information. Each consumer has a different way to handle the search for information. But there are similarities that make it easier for us to make information available about our games and our company. Here is where the public material makes a difference. Information should be easily available in order to lead a person who is interested in what we make to a positive buying decision. This means that information should be available both online and offline, in all the places where we expect consumers to search for information. Some of these sources we can control, such as company Web pages, social media and promotions; other we cannot, as, again, social media and reviews/ratings.

The third stage is the evaluation of alternatives, deciding between different games. How different alternatives are evaluated differs among consumers, and these processes do not even have to be perceived as logical. The more we know about this process, the better we can understand and communicate with our consumers. For games there seem to be three major sources for evaluating alternatives. The first one is word of mouth; what those close to the consumer think does matter a great deal. What trusted friends or colleagues think will have an impact on what games you choose to buy. The second is reviews and ratings from other consumers. In the age of metadata these numbers are easily gathered and posted online. The logic here seems to be that so-and-so many consumers cannot be wrong! Last but not least, a third source for evaluation is the brand, the studio that has developed the game. Again, this leads us back to the importance of making your brand *top of mind*.

The result of the evaluation of alternatives leads to the purchase decision, the actual purchase of a game.

The last stage, post-purchase behaviour, is unfortunately frequently overlooked or dismissed because of lack of knowledge of its importance. Once a consumer has bought a game, it is important that we recognize that we now have moved into a relationship of mutual agreement. Handled correctly, this can lead to more sales in the future. Two aspects are important once a consumer has bought a game (well, besides the fact that the game is considered fun): first, that the purchase be reconfirmed as being the right one and, second, that we support the consumer in his interaction with the game. Many of the promotions that are used communicate to those who have already bought the game that, yes, it was the right decision (more about promotion in Chapter 5). It is also important that the communication about the game, both before and after launch, be in line with what is offered so as to ensure that the expectations for the game are met. But, providing after-sales service to consumers is pivotal. There should be an organization that has the capacity to deal with the problems consumers experience, from problems with downloading or installing the game to content and billing. On several occasions the consumer will be frustrated when contacting the developer/publisher, and communicating with a frustrated consumer can be both hard and terrifying (most of us tend to avoid situations of conflict). But, each occasion the consumer decides to contact you and voice a complaint is an occasion where you have the possibility to reconnect and boost confidence.

When consumers buy

The last section in this chapter deals with when consumers buy games. This temporal dimension in consumer behaviour has two aspects. First, consumers buy games differently during the year; second, different consumers adopt new games and innovations differently.

Like any other cultural product, games are consumed differently over the year. This difference should be accounted for when you are planning release dates or other activities. The biggest sales are during Christmas, mostly as presents to others. But, a surprisingly large number of games are sold as presents to oneself! If games sold over Christmas are mostly intended as presents, it means that the buyer is probably not the person who will play the game. So communication during Christmas should be aimed at customers buying the games, not the consumer playing the game. You want the game to end up on the wish list! Other times when sales changes occur are during summer breaks and during long working vacations. This pattern is dependent on regional practices, so you are advised to know how the consumption patterns fluctuate on the platform you are selling your game on.

There are also the activities of other companies to keep in mind. What games are released that will compete with the game you are launching, probably in the same genre?

There are also individual differences in how consumers adapt to new games and new gaming technology. All products have a lifetime (more about this in Chapter 3), including games. This means that a game is played for a certain amount of time, after which it is placed in the far back of the shelf. Depending on the genre of game, this can be anything from a week (casual games) to years (Massively Multiplayer Online Role Playing Game, MMORPG). The same can

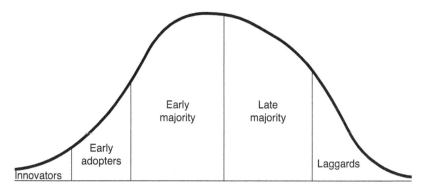

Figure 1.6 Diffusion of innovations

Source: Rogers, 1995

be said about new gaming technology. How fast consumers adapt both to games and technology differ.

During the lifetime of a game or gaming technology, there are five distinguishable types of consumers: innovator, early adopter, early majority, late majority and laggards. These different categories of consumers might all appreciate a game, but they all have different behaviours around when they decide to buy a game. Because of that, we have to communicate to these consumers differently.

Innovators are consumers who are always looking for new types of games. Many times these are very knowledgeable persons who take pride in knowing the ins and outs of games and gaming technology. Having the game first is extremely important for them.

Early adopters are consumers who also are among the first to buy new games. These consumers also form a larger set of persons who buy into a new game, meaning that they have an effect on how the game sells. Many of these are opinion leaders, meaning that others trust what they think about games and what games they buy.

The *early majority* are the consumers who buy new games when they are released. They do not depend on having it first, but they are interested in new games when they are released. These persons are also the first consumers who might look at reviews by other consumers. They want to make sure to buy a new game but also a good new game – as defined by opinion leaders.

The *late majority* are consumers who buy games when they are sure of the quality of the game. They are not pressed to buy a new game when it is released but would rather go with games that have high ratings and that they are sure they will enjoy playing.

Laggards are the sceptics of game consumers. These persons will buy a game only when it is part of mainstream – when enough people are playing the game to make it certain that they will enjoy it too.

The adaptation of new games and gaming technology suggests that we as marketers should plan for different consumers buying the game at different stages in the game's lifetime. A game that is considered obsolete by an *innovator* or *early adopter* could be desirable for the majority of game consumers.

Exercises

1   What kind of consumer are you developing games for? Do you know your gamers? How much do you know about them? Construct a profile of the person you are making games for, and make sure to include as many dimensions as possible about that person.
2   Take your favourite video game title and analyze its target audience. What is its target audience? Do you identify with this target audience? What do you think, having read this chapter, could have been done to market it better?
3   What type of gamer are you in terms of the diffusion of innovations model? Has your type evolved during the years? Can you apply this thinking to other types of game genres, specific game titles or gamer subcultures?

2 Marketing strategy and the marketing mix

In Chapter 2 we get into the thick of it and explore how a marketing strategy can be created and the usefulness of the marketing-mix tool in this process. We begin with the most basic starting point – ourselves and our company. From abstract to concrete we move from the company's mission to its objectives and goals and then to the actual result – the game portfolio. Games have a life cycle in the marketplace, and, depending on this general dimension, we can start creating a marketing strategy based on the underlying marketing mix.

Learning objectives

1   To learn the basic components of marketing strategy
2   To learn the process of creating a marketing plan using the marketing mix tool
3   To understand the relevance of company mission, objectives and goals for the process of marketing strategy
4   To establish the connection between game/product life cycles and marketing strategies

Introduction

Now that we have established the importance of knowing what customers you are developing games for and the number of dimensions these consumers can be defined by, it is time to have a look at the game developer company as a whole. It makes a lot of sense to start to develop games because you have a passion for games – as a matter of fact, we would argue that this is a necessity. It will show in your games, just as it will show in how you interact with your consumers. The founder and CEO of a major AAA studio in Sweden even went so far as to say that "we hire gamers, primarily – not skilled technicians". By this he meant that it is better to build technical skills to match your passion for games than the other way around. We could not agree more.

We argue that you have to be equally passionate about building a games company, one that goes beyond any single game idea. Once you have developed your first game, then what? Where are you heading, and how are you going to get there? We know that this one game start-up is how quite a few game developers are getting started. But the sooner you can start to figure out the bigger picture of your game developing, the better off you are. We deal with these questions and a few others in this chapter. Keep in mind that you might not be able to define all these aspects of your company at the outset; it is recommended that you keep them in mind and work them into your company once you have the information, knowledge and possibility to do so.

Company mission

All companies exist to accomplish something. That goes without saying. No matter whether we are talking about a car manufacturer, a restaurant, or a game developer. The more well defined this reason for being is, the better focus there will be in the company and the easier it will be for your company to communicate with consumers about what you are doing and why. Many conflicts in companies, internally between persons or externally about consumer expectations, can originate in different understandings of what the company is supposed to be doing and why. That is why it is important to define a *mission statement* for a company. This is a short definition of the purpose of the company, a statement that unifies internal efforts among those working in the company, builds the base for communication with consumers, and sets expectation from consumers. You might also want to view this mission statement as a social contract binding both the persons involved in the company and defining what you promise your consumers.

Mission statements from major game developers are for the most part well defined and continually used in both internal and external communication.

> "Dedicated to creating the most epic entertainment experiences . . . ever."
> Blizzard Entertainment

> "At Sony, our mission is to be a company that inspires and fulfills your curiosity."
>
> Sony

These mission statements are just examples. They should be meaningful for consumers in the context of these companies but also for motivating those employed by these companies and customers. In a sense these statements should convey why these companies exist. As you might have noticed, neither of these mission statements mentions specific products or services – what the companies actually do. Instead they are formulated more softly, describing what value the companies aim to create for their consumers. The reason for this is that there are many ways for these companies to create these values. Blizzard can create "epic entertainment experiences" in many ways, from games to accessories and huge events. As such, the mission statement sets the ambition of the company, not a definition of specific products.

It is recommended that a mission statement not include definitions of any products. The reason for this is that (as we get to in Chapter 3) what is offered by any company is mainly experiences, not products. Sony aims to inspire and fulfill your curiosity; thus its product line should enable just that. Blizzard Entertainment products should offer you epic entertainment experiences, whether through games or other products. So, focus on the benefit of the products – not the product itself.

One company that has used the value it has created to expand the products is Rovio, the maker of the game Angry Birds. Its mission statement reads, "Rovio is an entertainment media company, and the creator of the globally successful Angry Birds Franchise." Although this mission statement more defines who Rovio is at the moment than what its mission is for the future, notice that it does not define itself as a game developer, although it refers to its most successful game. Being an "entertainment media company" leaves the field open for Rovio to explore other media than games. That is why we are seeing films and amusement parks produced by Rovio.

Your mission statement thus addresses what value your organization intends to create – not specific products. An example that often is used when teaching marketing is the company Shell. In the 1980s this company defined itself as an oil company. Today it has redefined this and now defines itself as a company that provides energy. This redefinition has changed internally in terms of what kind of energy sources Shell is providing and also externally in terms of how it communicates with consumers and consumer expectations.

Company objectives and goals

The company mission statement might seem flimsy at first, soft and unspecific. The point is that it should inspire, both internally and externally, and point toward a direction the company is aiming at. With this mission at hand it then becomes a matter of defining objective and goals that are in line with the company mission. That is, how do we fulfill the mission statement of the company? The mission statement from Blizzard Entertainment does not say how the mission is to be achieved, although it directs further planning in that organization to make sure that whatever is undertaken it is in line with creating the "most epic entertainment experiences".

For Blizzard this mainly means developing video games, such as World of Warcraft, StarCraft or Diablo (this is of course just a guess, as we have not talked to them). Although developing games seems to be the objective of Blizzard, the mission statement does open up the possibility of other objectives as well, such as developing board games or action figures or hosting major events. As we write this book, the World of Warcraft movie has just been launched at cinemas all over the world and is similar to the direction taken by Rovio. The idea is that these activities all contribute to creating a "most epic entertainment experience". They are also in line with games, which is Blizzard's major product.

But, notice that there is nothing saying that Blizzard could not diversify into adventure parks or other products as long as these are in line with the mission statement.

This leads us into the concept of *diversification*. This is the process of producing products that are in line with the mission statement but different from the main product, the product that historically or conceptually is associated with the company. This can be successful. But it is well advised that the diversification be maintained in a way that the brand value is kept intact (more about brands in Chapter 4) and that it be in line with what consumers might expect from the company. Blizzard might succeed at building board games, but adventure parks could be a longer stretch. Breakfast cereals would definitely be unacceptable – it is hard to argue that breakfast cereals create the most epic entertainment experience. But keep in mind that at the end of the day it is consumers who decide whether the diversification is in line with the company's mission and whether they will embrace the new products or services.

When defining the goals of a company, it is important that these be both plausible and measurable. These two aspects make it possible for the whole company to come together in working toward its goals. Having plausible goals is important because there should be a shared understanding that we can do this! Goals should be visionary but still within reach. This relates to the second aspect. If goals are defined in such a way that they are measurable, it is possible to keep track of progress, bringing out the champagne when the goals are reached. There are many measurements that can be used for goals, but for a company in the game industry these would probably be defined by sales volume, market shares, user rating or expert ratings.

Keep in mind that goals are temporary, depending on where your company is at the moment, where it is coming from and where it is heading. A newly started developer might set a goal to achieve the necessary sales volume to fund its next game, while a more mature developer might define their goals by user ratings. There are, of course, possibilities to have several goals, but keep in mind that this can distort the goal image – so keep your eye on what is most important for you!

Both mission statement and objectives and goals are not something you work through at one point and then archive. Just as the world changes around game developers, these documents have to be the focus of frequent workshops and revisions in order to stay relevant for your consumers.

Game portfolio

It is now time to use your mission statement and the objective and goal that you have defined and turn them into something more tangible. This is where we start to plan for a game portfolio, a plan for what games should be developed and what strategic roles these games should play for the company. Or, if we use the same strategy as Rovio: what additional products should be part of what we offer to consumers? Now, we are well aware that most start-ups of game developers originate from a single game idea; from there a company starts taking shape. This company might very well be born out of necessity or from a strategic decision to host the development in a certain organizational form. Starting with a credible game idea that you have both the knowledge to develop and the passion to see through the whole development is good. What we would like to add is that sooner or later you should think about how your game ideas fit together, as a game portfolio. And here is where the strategic work comes in, both to find new game projects for the intended consumer and to make sure these are in line with your company strategy

For smaller game developers, a game portfolio might make little sense, as developers usually move from one production to the next, depending on what can be funded and gain the attention of publishers. In that sense, game portfolios, it could be argued, are more useful for publishers, which have the strategic position to fund and publish games that are within their mission. But, although you as a developer are not looking at a portfolio of games, it is well worth the effort to map out how the games you are making fit into the portfolio of the company, as well as those of the publishers you are working with or game pitching ideas to.

Boston Consulting Group have developed a matrix that is useful for thinking about the game portfolio, called the BCG growth–share matrix. Using the two dimensions of the relative market shares individual games have and the growth rate of those specific markets, we can divide the matrix into four distinguishable fields or strategic business units (SBUs). These fields contain games that in the BCG matrix are called *question marks, stars, cash cows* and *dogs.*

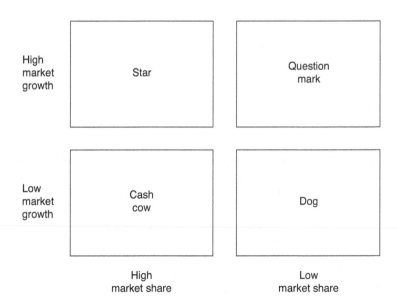

Figure 2.1 The BCG growth-share matrix

Source: Boston Consulting Group

A *question mark* is a game that does not have much market share. This means that the game does not sell much compared to other games in the same genre. It might even be a game that has not yet been released, a game that still is under development. But the game is developed for a market that is fairly big and also a market that is growing. This market could be defined by geographical boundaries, genre or other distinguishable factors. An example is a first-person shooter, not yet released but in a market that has a high growth rate. At this point it is unsure what will become of the game – it is a question mark.

A *star* is a game that, just like the question mark, is developed for a market with high growth. But, unlike the question mark, this game has high market share, meaning that it has high sales numbers. High sales in a growing market! As such, the star is truly a star! In an ideal case this is what the question mark will become once it has been launched. For games the first days or weeks are many times indicative of the overall sales. Being featured on a marketplace like the App Store has the potential to generate sales. The video game industry is a hit-driven industry, just like the majority of cultural industries. This means that developing games that will be stars is something that most game developers and publishers are aiming at. This in turn creates a market where competition among starts is fierce.

A *cash cow* is a game that, just like the star, has high sales, but unlike the star it operates in a market that is marked by low growth. Games that are positioned here are generating money and considered the cash cows for companies. For many companies these games are what continue to make money, funding the development of new games – of new question marks. Cows are thus still having high sales but in a market that may be saturated in the future, since they are selling in markets that are not growing. This might be genres that are no longer that attractive or regions where game sales are low in general. Cows may have been stars at one point in time and kept their relative market share as general market growth slowed down. One should thus not underestimate the value of having cows in your game portfolio. They might not attract as much publicity as the stars, they might not be as hyped – but they generate valuable funds for your company.

A *dog* is a game that operates on a market with low growth rate, just like the cow. But, unlike the cow, the dog is not selling. The relative market shares are low and there are several other titles that sell much better. This means that a dog is not generating any money, maybe not even enough to sustain the after-sales service required in forums, technical issues and consumer service. On top of that, the market for the game might even be going down! The dog is then a slow-selling game in a shrinking market. It seems that dogs are useless, something one should put to sleep. But there are some aspects of these mutts that we should not underestimate. That game might draw the attention of consumers to other games. The game might be low maintenance, meaning that it remains in a marketplace and there are no costs associated with keeping it alive. Our experience is that dogs are hard to close down because of sunk costs; the money you have put into the game becomes an irrational argument for spending more money on sustaining it. If there are no reasons for keeping the dog around – stop supporting it.

The BCG matrix should be used as a tool to help you think and plan. Mapping out existing games on the grid can provide a good overview on where the different games in your game portfolio or in the portfolio of a potential publisher are located. It is important that this be viewed as a tool for strategic decisions. In general it is beneficial if there are games in each category of the matrix, because the matrix has a flowchart character (following the game life cycle, described later). Usually new games start out as question marks during development, ideally become stars after launch, in time slow down and become cows and eventually become dogs. If there are games along this path it means that the company is creating games that have different strategic positions, from new productions that it hopes will be stars to cows that have the possibility to fund new projects. But we should not underestimate the dog. Although there is a need to kick the dog out if it is not sustainable to fund it, the dog can also be revitalized in order to improve its lifetime. This is the effect of releasing patches and expansion packs.

Game life cycle

It goes without saying that a game does not have an infinite lifetime. Some games are played longer than others, but sooner or later a game loses its gamers. All games thus follows similar cycles of launch and fade-out. This is called the life cycle of games. In Chapter 1 we described the diffusion of innovations that explains the different types of consumers who interact with a new product at different stages. In general products go through four different phases in their lifetime: introduction, growth, maturity, and decline.

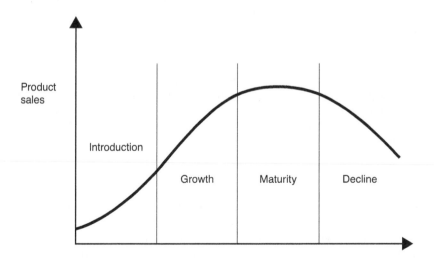

Figure 2.2 Game life cycle

The first phase of any game is development. Although there are no possibilities for consumers to buy the game during this period, there are a number of different market communication activities that should take place during this period in order to create strong expectations, to communicate that the game is coming and to promote it and get attention and feedback from gamers and the press. The stars of the BCM matrix can be found here. Consumers who are understood as innovators (see Chapter 1) many times show a great deal of interest in games under development, both how they are developed and how to get access to the game when it first launches.

At some point the game is introduced to consumers. Usually, this is the point when the game is launched. But we all know that there are several different contact points with consumers during production, alpha- and beta-launches not the least. Plus, there are possibilities for soft launches, which reach a limited number of consumers. Once a game is introduced, it is available to consumers: to the innovators and early adopters of the game.

Once the game is introduced, it is expected that the sales will grow and that the game will attract more consumers. This growth phase is the point when the early majority starts buying the game. Often this period is critical for exposure to attract as many gamers as possible. It is also at this point that it is possible to decide whether the game is having the start that you were hoping for or if the sales are low and the game is not reaching the sales goal.

As the game reaches its maturity, it also attracts the late majority of gamers. For most games this is also the longest period. The game has passed the initial hype, and sales in the long run will slow. How many days or weeks can the game stay in the top sales ranking? Once the game has matured, it is possible to evaluate how good a cash cow it is. Does it have the possibility to generate funds during a longer time? Did the game outlive the initial craze?

At some point the sales of all games decline. Consumers might still enjoy playing the game, but revenues from sales, subscription and in-game purchases decline. There are still the laggards who generate some revenue streams, but the decline is a reality. We now have a dog on our hands, and it is important to make a decision. In an ideal case, if you have a well-planned game portfolio, there will be a replacement game at this point, whether patches on your existing game, such as World of Warcraft (Blizzard Entertainment/Activision) and Candy Crush (King), or new games such as the Call of Duty franchise (Activision). This will stretch the life cycle of your game and game portfolio.

Marketing mix

Now that we have worked through the company strategy and game portfolio, it is time to have a more specific look at the *marketing strategy*. The marketing strategy is how the company is going to create value for consumers. This, at the end of the day, should be the goal of any developer – making games that can be enjoyed and make a difference in the hands on the consumers. As we have described in the introduction to this book, marketing is much more than

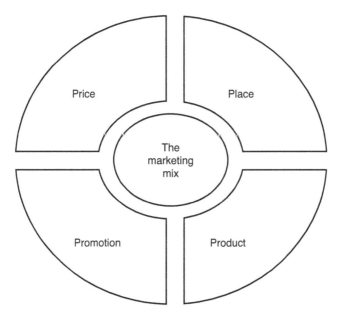

Figure 2.3 4Ps

promotion, although this is many times how it is talked about and described. But promotion is only part of the *marketing mix.*

When the concept of marketing mix was introduced, it was framed as a way to conceptualize the soup of marketing, what spices you put into that soup and how that tasted. And, as we all know, we like our soups tasting good! Originally there were twelve different ingredients, but these have now been boiled (*sic*) down to four: *product, price, place* and *promotion*. These are most of the times referred to as the 4Ps of marketing.

Each of these variables within the marketing mix contains much information about that specific area and can be a way for your company to excel and differentiate itself from competitors. A *product* is what the company is developing, from the quality and design of the game to packaging and after-sales service. The *price* contains list price, discounts and payment methods. *Place* refers to the different channels through which the games are to be sold, logistics of physical games and/or platform for digital distribution. *Promotion*, in the end, contains the advertising, sales promotion and public relations that are planned. In Chapter 5 we will get back to these variables of the marketing mix in detail. What we want to argue here is the importance of developing an integrated marketing mix specifically for your company. This means that there has to be a strong correlation among product, price, place and promotion (the 4Ps). The consumer should, in the ideal case, understand these variables are coherent and supporting a unified front from a developer. This also has to be connected to the mission statement of the company. This is the coherence of a company with a strong strategy.

In order to conceptualize the importance of an integrated marketing mix, let us have a look at two different strategies. Both developer A and B have been established quite recently, and both are to embark upon the adventure of building games they are passionate about. But how they develop their marketing mix is quite different. Developer A set out to build smaller, casual games. They plan to have a continuous stream of smaller games that take a short time to develop. Quite contrary to this, developer B set out to develop a major game that will shoot like a star and have huge sales and success (yes, both strategies are quite common). How these developers relate to the 4Ps would be quite different.

Developer A, already having defined their product as casual games, would be looking at selling their games for a lower price. This could also include giving it away and using in-game purchases to make a profit. The places for this game would probably be mobile platforms or social media and browsers. As for promotion, this would probably be limited to word of mouth, community building online and banners on some strategically chosen Web pages.

So what about developer B? As you understand by now, since the product is quite different from developer A's, we would also expect the other variables to be in line with that difference. Developer B, who is going for the AAA game, would need to have a presence in the major markets for games, both physical and digital markets. The game would need to be vastly expanded in scale compared to a casual game in order to compete with other AAA games and meet the expectations of consumers of what a AAA game is. As for promotion, you would also expect massive exposure, trailers in public media and PR in the international press.

The point here is not that the one strategy is better than the other. All developers have different financial and technical possibilities to develop games that will create both possibilities and limitations. But the strategies you use to develop your marketing "soup" have to be consistent with what you are delivering in order for you to create games that can attract consumers and fulfill expectations.

On top of the 4Ps of marketing, it has been suggested that as society is transformed into one in which services became more important, we have to understand the market mix using three additional ingredients: physical evidence, personnel and process. Yes, they all start with P. Together these aspects are referred to as the 7Ps of the service marketing mix. In Chapter 3 we discuss the relationships between products and services and how understanding video games as services changes our perceptions. When delivering services there are additional spices that have to be part of your marketing soup. The reason for this is that you are dealing more with consumers in creating long-term relationships, as you want the consumer to come back.

We believe that physical evidence is the one factor that is less useful for game development. Basically this deals with how your company provides physical evidence of the quality of your service. Since quality is intangible, it is helpful to add physical proof to something that is hard to evaluate. A classic example here is the old architecture of banks: marble pillars, shiny floors and bars in front of the cashiers. These aspects were supposed to communicate how safe it was to keep your money in the bank. So maybe the evidence for a gaming experience would be a real-life token handed out only to the best of the best: a pin, medal, sunglasses or any other visible item.

When dealing with consumers, you are dependent on your personnel: taking phone calls, answering mail, posting in forums or meeting your consumers face to face. This means that you need to have a strategy for choosing the persons who have this contact. They are, in a very real sense, the face of your company in every encounter with your consumers. These persons should then have the ability to embody the mission statement of your company when communicating with consumers. If your company is defined as playful, offering playful games, your personnel should communicate this!

The last aspect in the process of delivering a service is the process in which you are delivering it. The prime example of this process is what you encounter when visiting McDonald's. It is said that the encounter should be the same no matter where you are in the world. Through a standardized process they are trying to ensure the best service encounter. We are not encouraging you to adopt a McDonaldization of consumer interaction in the video game industry, but the example highlights the importance of having a clear strategy for how you interact with consumers and through what processes. Again, this process should reflect your company values and objectives.

The world's shortest marketing plan

The input from the marketing mix can form the basics for developing a marketing plan. This plan is a document that maps out where you are positioned at the moment but also highlights areas that need to be clarified or defined. The most important aspect of a marketing plan is the work that goes into making one. This enables all the persons in the organization to agree on a direction for the company. Just as with any strategic document, it is equally important that the result not be something you only put in a folder and archive. A plan should be implemented and evaluated in cycles to make sure that you are on track and are positioning your company and resources where they are most needed.

There are many forms for marketing plans. When searching for marketing plans on the Internet you will find that there are an almost unlimited number of templates and consultancy companies offering to help. Our suggestion is that the persons who are involved in making the games and in running the company be very much involved in order to get relevant information and commitment to the plan. For this purpose we have found it useful to use the World's Shortest Marketing Plan.

When breaking down all four dimensions of the marketing mix into questions that challenge different aspects, you are forced to start making sense of your company. Some of these questions may be easy to answer, while other may be harder. But providing answers to all questions will in the end enable you to form a coherent and sound marketing plan.

	What	**Why**	**When**	**How**	**How much**	**Who**
Product	What products do you sell?	What need does it fill?	When do you need it?	How will the product fill the need?	Product cost, volume to be sold etc.	Customer segments to be targeted?
Price	What price will you sell for?	Why is that the right price?	How long will the price be valid?	How will the price develop over time?	How much sales and margin will be created?	Different prices for different segments?
Place	How will products be distributed?	Why choose these channels?	When do customer choose different channels?	How will our creations enter these channels?	What are the cost/benefits of these channels?	How do different segments use different channels?
Promotion	What type of promotion to be used?	Why choose these activities?	Timing: launch, lifecycle etc.	How will the promotion be executed?	Cost/benefit of the promotion?	Target group for various promotions?

Figure 2.4 The world's shortest marketing plan

Source: Kelly O'Dell

SWOT

Game developers are all part of the ecology of the video game industry. This means that you will have to relate to the environment in which your organization exists in order to build your company. There are different kinds of organizations you will have to relate to, stakeholders that also have an interest in your organization: government agencies, trade agencies, competitors and collaborators.

The SWOT model is a tool that will help you to think about your company in terms of strength, weakness, opportunities and threats. The benefit of this model is that it also takes into account the ecology in which your company operates. No company operates as a lonely island, although some might act that way. Whatever you do is a result of your position, and whatever you do will have an effect on your stakeholders.

There are two dimensions of the SWOT model: internal information about your company and external information about the market you operate in. This means that there are factors that will affect only your company and those that will have a wider impact. Strength and weaknesses thus concern your company. What resources do you possess that have the possibility of leading to a competitive advantage? Do you have skills or knowledge that other companies do not have? Remember that strengths and weaknesses are not absolute; they are relative to those of your competitors. If you, for example, have a motion capture studio, this will become a strength only if your competitors experience the absence of one as a weakness. Another example is being extremely proficient in coding C++ (or any other relevant language). This is a strength if your competition lacks this skill. But if most of your competitors are extremely proficient at

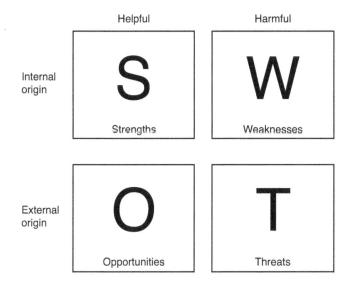

Figure 2.5 SWOT model

coding, you have no competitive advantage in that area. The same concerns the weaknesses of your company.

In any market there are opportunities and threats. These are technical, political, cultural and other movements that will affect your company as well as your competitors. The shortage of RAM memory did at one point affect the whole computer industry, just as the tax breaks offered by Montreal and Quebec affected the video game industry. Some of these major movements can be foreseen; then it is a matter of how you handle them. Others you cannot foresee and thus cannot plan for. It is important to eliminate threats that you know of at this point.

In order to develop your company using a SWOT model, you are dependent on information. Most of the information concerning your organization should be fairly easy to produce, although information about competitors and other stakeholders is harder to come by. But compared to ten or twenty years ago it is much easier today to use digital information to build a SWOT model. There are national public data about public organizations that in most countries are available online. There is also much information available through trade papers, interviews and trade organization. The challenge here is twofold: turning data into knowledge that is useful for a SWOT and evaluating the validity of the data you retrieve.

With the SWOT completed, the next step is to create a list of actions, based on what you have defined in each of the boxes: strength, weaknesses, opportunities and threats. How do you further exploit your strengths, avoid your weaknesses and seize the opportunities by evading the threats? There is also an optional next step to the analysis, called the SWOT plus, in which weaknesses are supposed to be (partially) counterbalanced by the strengths and threats by opportunities. If this achievable, then your business will be well prepared for the challenges of the future.

To end this chapter we would like to offer a gem from a politician. In 2002 the US secretary of defense Donald Rumsfeld pondered the reality of knowledge and offered us an interesting view. He claimed that: "Reports that say that something hasn't happened are always interesting to me, because as we know, there are known knowns; there are things we know we know. We also know there are known unknowns; that is to say we know there are some things we do not know. But there are also unknown unknowns – the ones we don't know we don't know. And if one looks throughout the history of our country and other free countries, it is the latter category that tend to be the difficult ones."

Exercises

1 Have you considered formulating your game studio's mission, objectives and goals? If not – now is a perfect time to exploring these questions! They're more important than it seems. What did you discover?
2 Using the world's shortest marketing plan as described earlier, create a plan for your game project. What kind of new insight did this exercise produce?
3 Do a SWOT analysis of your game studio and then a separate analysis of your game project. What is the result? How do they differ? Compare your results with a SWOT of a game developer that you admire.

3 Video games as products or services

In this chapter we introduce the necessary step of analyzing the core of your offering – the game. This is in line with what we have discussed regarding the marketing mix and its emphasis on the first P – the product. We'll learn that product is not the only way to view games but rather that they exist on a spectrum between products and services. This redefinition of games as (in some sense) services opens up a new perspective on how we should develop and market games and, most important, also suggests that experiences become a central dimension of the entire process. These experiences are based on expectations and can also take into consideration when repositioning the game experience to improve the marketing of game projects.

Learning objectives

1   To understand the difference between a product and service and what this entails for game development
2   To understand how the analysis of experiences can be incorporated as a unifying perspective on game development and marketing
3   To understand the relevance of expectations and how these can be integrated into a marketing strategy

Introduction

Now that we have laid out the basics of the market for video games and the strategic marketing decisions your game company has to be involved in, it is time to look more closely at the video game itself. As this is a book on marketing, not game development, we assume that you are more knowledgeable about creating games than we are. We also assume that you have been involved in several projects during your education or professional career. No matter the project, these have given you experience in what it takes to make a game. For this chapter we ask you to take a step back to get some distance on how you conceive games while making them and to look at games as an offering to consumers. The better you can define what you are developing and why, the better you can communicate this to potential consumers.

A product perspective on games

It is said that we today live in a consumer society; this means that to a large extent we heavily depend on products and services in our daily lives. It also means that we define who we are and who we want to be through consumption (more about this in Part II), for example by having the right fashion, gadgets or cars. Much of what we buy and consume actually has very little to do with surviving and is more associated with experiencing pleasure and the feeling of joy. Whereas we (as in, us living in developed countries) used to buy in order to obtain the necessities of life, today we mostly buy for the experience of buying and using; many of us have already acquired the basics for living.

On the surface, this also seems to be what games are all about – but it goes deeper than that. Much of what we consume has to do with experiencing that thrill of consuming, the joy of a new pair of sneakers or those new headphones. The bottom line is that much of what we do and experience on a daily basis has to do with our interaction with products that are offered to us. Today, we might rephrase the French philosopher Descartes's saying "I think therefore I am," instead shouting from the rooftops "I shop therefore I am" (but more about this in the postmodern consumer in Chapter 7).

Products then can be defined as anything that can be put on a market for others to acquire, something that will satisfy the wants or needs of those consumers. This includes everything from clothes, cars and phones to milk (we're not letting go of this fine example of a product yet) and games. Broadly defined, products are all those tangible, material things we can acquire from other actors: shops, organizations or companies. Traditionally, marketing has been preoccupied with products – as you might recall from Chapter 2, one of the 4Ps is the product, and actually it is the first one, signalling an implicit assumption that marketing deals with physical goods. What's more, another P – place – also reveals the same assumption that marketing deals with products that are sold in physical stores. Actually the historical origins of the marketing discipline are in logistics and distribution, since marketing in the early industrialized market economy meant transporting products from factories to (re)sellers. To this day, in many (big) corporations logistics/distribution and marketing are the same division or closely aligned to large extent.

It is quite easy to place games in the category of products. Traditionally this has always been the case. In other publishing industries, a game, a song or a story is produced – inscribed onto a medium that can be transported to a consumer in a business transaction: a disc, a CD, a book or another form. When we conceive of games as products, this affects how we understand and build games and relationships with the consumer. In the strictest sense, delivering a high-quality game to a consumer should be the main goal of this transaction. Notice that the view on games as products also means that the transaction ends when the transaction has been made. Sold – gone, moving on! As a matter of fact, during most of its history the game industry structure has been defined by the *physical* distribution chain. Resellers, distributors and, by extension, game publishers all wielded influence over the industry by controlling the physical distribution chain of video games.

For many years one of the biggest game publisher in the world – Electronic Arts (EA) – based its success on controlling and integrating the entire physical distribution chain. EA also very early on realized the leverage of marketing – but this was built on control from everything from CD/DVD packaging facilities and local distributors to point-of-sales merchandising, bundled game deals, share of local marketing or media/promotion budgets and so on up and down the distribution chain. The same applies for the traditional game console business model, which has always been built on a physical distribution model that keeps a global network of stakeholders with vested interest as fairly stable business model of physical game sales. Swiftly migrating the entire game console business model to a purely digital distribution model, which has been proposed by many game industry pundits since the dawn of the mainstream consumer Internet in the mid-1990s, would not only upset thousands of powerful distributors and resellers but also undermine the power base and stability of the entire business model. Major electronics retailer chains would not make profits on game console sales, and all the game retailers of the world would have to shut down. Therefore, paradoxically, the video game industry – the first truly digital global media industry – has been one of the slowest of all major media industries to digitize its distribution and business models. The migration to a digital distribution model has already mostly been achieved – major game retailer chains have gone bankrupt because of competition from digital distribution and/or online stores, and all console platforms offer digital distribution options of some sort. Despite all of this, all the game console platforms still rely on physical media and their distribution.

A service perspective on games

As you might realize by now, this is not what the game industry looks like today. Nor is it how other publishing industries look. The value chain of the video game industry has changed dramatically since the turn of the century, from a trade of physical products to digital trade handled through online services. A business transaction from a seller to a consumer is always part of a continuous relationship between the seller and buyer. A point sale of one game is, the seller hopes, made as part of a continuous chain of purchases. Most consumers do not buy only one game but buy games continuously throughout their gaming years.

There are also reasons to re-evaluate games as products if we look at what a game is (here we want to emphasize that we do not aim to contribute to the many philosophical discussions of what a game is). If we loosen the definition of products, we have the possibility of seeing the many dimensions of consumer offerings – where products and services are parts of the experience.

A service is defined along four dimensions: it is (1) intangible, (2) inseparable, (3) variable and (4) perishable. *Intangible* means that there is nothing physical about a service. When you are playing the game, it is the game setting, the narrative and the features that you interact with – none of which are physical, although you do need physical products to access the game. These physical products will define the game you as a developer create, but the game itself can be understood as a service. The experience of playing a game is also *inseparable* from the gamer. Your presence in the game and other gamers' presence in the game change the product. The experience of playing a game is thus dependent on the consumer, and different consumers have different experiences. *Variable* means that a service will be delivered differently each time you engage with it. Mainly this depends on it being persons delivering services. Although in games we meet both NPC (Non-player characters) and other gamers. This means that the idea is that each gaming session will be different, depending on other gamers. The last one, *perishable*, means that there is no way for you to store a service, to be used in the future. What games do very well if to offer environments that can be experiences again and again, although this might give you an impression that you can store an experience for later, actually the each gaming session is unique and can only be experience there and then because of its dependence of other gamers and your actions.

A service can thus be defined as any activity or set of activities that can be offered in a market for others to acquire that will satisfy the wants or needs of these consumers. This includes activities like hotel nights, a haircut, a dinner at a restaurant or (again) a game. The main difference between a product and a service is that products are tangible, while a service is intangible. Yes, there are sometimes tangible aspects involved in a service encounter, but there is no tangible take-away from that meeting. A product can also be stored for later usage, something that is not possible for a service. A flight seat (not the actual seat as such but the renting of that seating space during a particular flight, sold as an "airline ticket"), for example, cannot be stored for later usage. When the plane takes off, it is gone. A service is then something that we engage in just as much as we engage with products, if not more. Since the 1980s service industries have seemed to be growing more rapidly than product-based industries.

The difference between a product and a service is not always clear. And most offerings we are exposed to contain both products and services. The difference should be understood as a scale, from pure goods to pure services (see figure 3.1). There are very few pure products and services; most offerings are somewhere in the middle. Pure goods are products such as timber or salt; examples of pure services, in contrast, include some forms of consultancy.

It matters if an offering is categorized as a service or a product. Changing our perception from games as products to games as service highlights the continuous relationship with the consumer. In a sense we are letting them into our digital worlds where they are exposed to different challenges and social relations. This setting is something we improve continuously.

The differences between a product and a service then lead us to two observations when it comes to games. The first one is that instead of looking at these two offerings separately, we need to focus on what kind of experiences are offered. This means that in any (almost) offering there are both product and

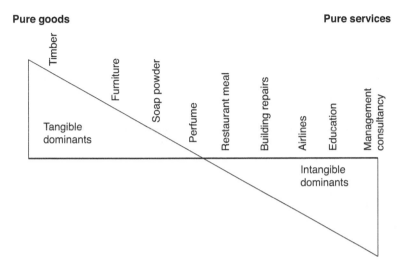

Figure 3.1 Scale of market entities

Source: Shostack, 1977, p. 77

service dimensions, but a too-narrow focus on the specific product or service makes us miss the reason why a person chooses to buy a specific game. If we move from the product/service categories and look instead at experiences, we can appreciate bundles of offerings (products and/or services) that offer the experiences sought by the consumer. The second is that a game is a unique case that renders the differences rather obsolete – it can be conceived as either a product or a service. Focusing on games as product misses the point – but so does focusing on games only as services. The fact is that games are made into being different things, by different games companies – either as a service to interact in online environments, or as a point-sale of a game product.

While it may come as a surprise to many that games can be framed as services, as a matter of fact most digital media today have already made the transformation from a product-dominant perspective to a service-dominant perspective. For the first two decades of the PC software industry, software was something that was sold in a box. Product launches of new operating systems, such as Windows 95, were always accompanied by nice images of software CD-ROMs in packages rolling off production lines in some unknown "software factory" somewhere. Nowadays we live in the age of the "app", and the biggest software products in the world have all turned into service-based business models – so-called software as a service (SaaS). Adobe no longer sells its famous Creative Suite of software products, but since 2013 they sell the Creative Cloud, where consumers pay for the software *service* of the previous software products but with added SaaS features such as continuous upgrades, cloud storage and collaboration tools. If we consider most successful smartphone global apps, few of those are *not* linked to Internet/cloud-based SaaS infrastructure. Game apps initially managed to create profitable revenue streams based on a product-like one-off purchase business model, but this was very swiftly replaced by the more successful "freemium" in-app purchases business model with SaaS characteristics. In this model the app is for free and most of the gaming experience is provided free, but upgrades and more advanced features are not, acting as a type of "optional subscription service" where most active consumers buy premium features amounting to at least the price of a one-off purchase and in many cases substantially more. Digital music sales were pioneered by Apple's iTunes Music Store, where one-off purchases of single songs and albums that in encrypted format were "owned" by the consumer on his or her computer or iPod hard drive – until music subscription services such as Spotify, Pandora, Rdio, Deezer and others ushered in a SaaS business model that is replacing the product-based business model and forcing Apple to launch its own music SaaS, called Apple Music. There are many more examples and all of these industry examples show that service-dominant business models are not only abstractions.

Moments of truth for your (service) company

Defining a game as a service has implications for how you deliver it to consumers. In order to deliver consumer experiences that are dependent both on the persons in your company that your consumers meet and how consumers interact with the game, you need to set up your organization to support a service-focused approach. A service focus does not mean that the consumer is always right, but it means that your job is to make sure that the consumer can have the best experience possible with your services – with your games. Consumers, then, are then not burdens when they contact you or when they turn to you to complain.

Each meeting with a consumer is a possibility for you to communicate with and improve the experience of that consumer, even when the consumer turns to you to complain. When a consumer has a bad experience using your game (there might be a bug!), he or she has two choices: exit or voice. Exit means that the consumer chooses to leave, not playing your game more. The reason for this choice will never reach you. You will notice only the exit. But if a consumer chooses voice, he or she starts a dialogue with you – "I've found a bug and it limits my gaming experience!" This enables you to both correct the problem and regain that consumer's expectation of a good experience through you and your games. You might think that one consumer who complains is no problem. But you can be sure that that consumer will share the experience with his or her friends, both online and offline. This is the power of word of mouth that we describe more about in Chapter 5.

Jan Carlzon, who was the CEO of SAS Group, the biggest airline company in Northern Europe in the 1980s and early 1990s, wrote a book in which he coined the term "the moment of truth". This concept highlights the value of gearing an organization toward delivering great service experiences in all meetings with the consumer. For Jan Carlzon, every meeting with the consumer was a moment of truth, a moment where the company's representative could deliver a great experience – if he or she was enabled by the organization. In the original Swedish, this book's title in translation is *Tear down the pyramids*. In order to deliver great service there is a need to rethink organizational structure and organizational logic and philosophies. Traditionally an organization is conceptualized in charts as a pyramid, with the CEO at the top and the persons who actually interact with the consumer at the bottom. This builds on the assumption that the organization is geared to carrying out directions from the CEO. The organization supports the CEO in his or her work. But the CEO is rarely the one who interacts with the consumer! So from a service perspective the organizational pyramid should be turned upside down. The organization ought to be set up to support the persons who interact with the consumers, both structurally, in how these persons best can meet consumers, and ideologically, in terms of the power they have to make decisions aimed at helping consumers. So what are your moments of truth in your organization, and how is your organization geared to handle these?

Consumer expectations

If games are understood as services, the concept of consumer expectation becomes relevant to incorporate in any marketing work in your organization. This is saying not that products are less important when it comes to expectations but that services offer you continuous possibilities to build and meet expectations. It is claimed that we today live in an expectations society, that we face on a daily basis many marketing messages that try to communicate to us what to expect from service X or product Y. Consumer expectations should not be neglected when it comes to making games.

Much of marketing communications (see Chapter 5) is about setting expectations, just as a strong brand creates expectations (more about this in Chapter 4). And building expectations for a game before it is launched is sound marketing strategy. There is strong evidence from research that high expectations for a game that is about to be launch have the effect of improving overall consumer evaluations of the game.

Before a game is launched there are, in general, two different modes that the game can be evaluated on – high expectations and low expectations. These expectations can come from many different factors: perhaps the developer previously has released successful or poor games, or the game studio has a strong or weak brand and reputation or the developer has pursued an intensive promotion campaign to increase the game's exposure. No matter the reason, from a marketing perspective it is always important to create high expectations before launch. The reason for this is that the actual experience of the game will be a result of the position to which you have managed to elevate the consumer, positive or negative.

The difference between expectations for a game and the evaluation of the game is the game itself. If you have high expectations for a game that is launched,

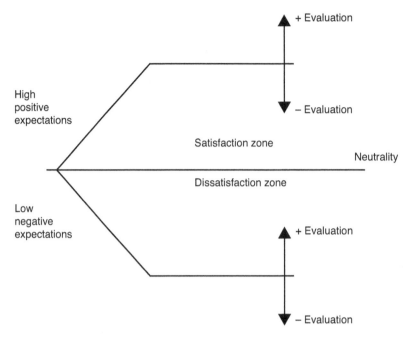

Figure 3.2 Consumer expectations

Source: Oliver, 1997, pp. 115–117

the consumers' overall evaluation of the game will be elevated. The same happens with low expectations – the consumers' overall evaluation of the game will be lowered. The results are that evaluations of games are dependent on previous expectations of the game. Compared to a situation where there are no expectations, either positive or negative expectations will affect the evaluation as it increases or decreases the point of departure. A negative evaluation of a game will thus still be a positive evaluation if the consumer has high expectations; and the opposite, a positive evaluation of a game still risks a negative evaluation if there are low expectations.

The takeaway from the consumer expectations research is that generating high expectations always seems to be beneficial for the overall evaluation of a game. The success of a game has everything to do with having your company move toward being a service company that creates consumer expectation and meet expectations.

Layers of an experience

The experience of interacting with games or any other offering can be defined as consisting of three different layers. The first layer deals with the *core* of the offering. When approaching a new game project, it is suggested that you frame this in a manner that will draw out what is actually offered through the game. What is it that consumers are meant to experience when interacting with the game? Simply put, why should they buy the game? With other types of products we could be looking at practical problems that could be solved – for example transportation. Although there are special aspects of certain games – one to create a learning platform to teach calculus, for example – most video games offer the possibility to experience different kind of feelings: being scared, feeling brave, being excited and so on. On top of this you have the social aspects: creating friends, socializing, joining a team.

Here, again, is where the mission of the company comes into play. If a company like Blizzard is offering the most epic entertainment, then that should be at the core. The dangers in defining your core offering as a product/service are that, first, you will be stuck offering that kind of product and, second, that the product/service is actually only a vehicle for you to bring an experience to your consumer.

This brings us to the second level. This level deals with the actual *experience*, as developed from the core. With the core of the experience firmly defined, it is inscribed into a product or service that it can be delivered and communicated

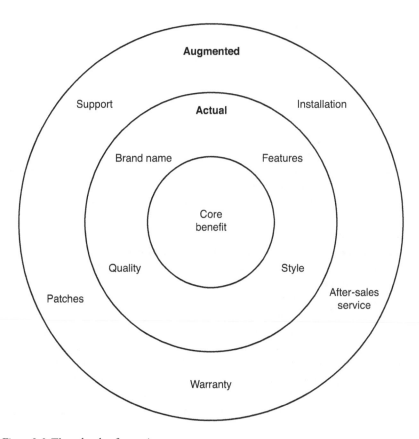

Figure 3.3 Three levels of experiences

to a consumer. An epic entertainment experience can be delivered through a wide array of products or services, although what most of us have seen this far are games. This is the benefit of understanding a game as the materialization of what core experience the company wants to offer. This opens up the possibility of offering other products that have the same values.

Both King and Blizzard are unique examples of the core values of a company being materialized into other products and not only games. Yes, there is Candy Crush and World of Warcraft, but there are also films. But the main part of game developers is nowhere near the position of these companies. Our argument is that although you are developing games for millions you still benefit from keeping track of how your core values are developed into actual products. On a general level, distinguishing what you want to offer the consumer from the actual games enables you to think beyond the game and to what the consumers are supposed to experience.

The third level of an experience is the *augmented experience*. These are additional products and services that are attached to your game in order to improve the experience. These can be continual updates, consumer services and different kind of discounts on other games. In short, it is all the extra things that you get when you buy a game. Most developers and publishers have at this point understood the value of adding a layer that makes the consumers' interaction with games and gaming easier. Having access to support and updates, for example, keeps the consumer in the loop and improves the overall experience.

When it is understood that an offering to consumers consists of more than the actual product/service, it becomes evident that the dimensions of your offering are far more extensive than you previously assumed. Relating to these dimensions, you can both position your games toward the vision of your company and also differentiate them from your competitors'. There are quite a few companies that have set up as their core business idea to offer entertainment and leisure activities – everything from movies to music and video games. This means that, in a sense, all of these companies could potentially compete with game developers, because they compete for the same total combined budget that consumers spend on leisure activities. What differentiates all these companies is, among other things, that they have decided to construct different actual products for consumers' fun and leisure time. This brings us to the next level of competition, between companies that make the same product – games. Most consumers do at this level differentiate between different games, depending on their gaming preferences. But if a consumer has a problem differentiating products, companies also compete with augmented products. Which has the best service deal? Which offers the most additional services via subscription? And so on.

Think about other products that are similar, for example insurance or a particular model of car sold by different dealers. By offering an additional dimension of service, it is possible to differentiate yourself from your competitors. There is then competition between companies, in all three dimensions. Making a strategic decision on how to relate to your competition is in the interest of all game developers.

Repositioning the game experience

Getting the right product out on the right market is something that might take both patience and time. There are two reasons why you should reconsider your position: either the game life cycle has started to decline (see Chapter 2) or your game is having a hard time selling in the first place. In either of these cases there is a need to rethink what you are doing.

When repositioning a game, there are two dimensions that are important to consider: game and market. The game can be modified to incorporate improvements in order to attract consumers, just as a market is never something given. A market is something that you can construct, choose and modify. Depending on your analysis of why the game is not selling, there are four choices for repositioning available to you (see figure 3.4).

The four strategies that you can employ are: market penetration, game development, market development and diversification. A *market penetration* strategy means that you continue to pursue working with a current game for the current market. It might be that you have a great game for a specific segment of consumers, but you might not have had enough exposure (see Chapter 5). Your potential market shares on this could be much higher, if only consumers were aware of the game! In this case your strategy is all about exposure to gain market shares, to increase the number of consumers who buy your game.

A *game development* strategy means that you are selling your game in a market that you want to attract, the segment that you have identified as the target for your game. But there is a difference between games that gain a high share of this market and your game. It could be a result of a miscalculation about what features to include in the development of the game. Or it might be that a game is declining and no longer contains relevant features for that segment. In this case your strategy is about product development. What do you need to do with your game in order to attract the targeted market? One of the most common features to use is patches, or expansion packs. These prolong the life cycle of the game and help maintain market share.

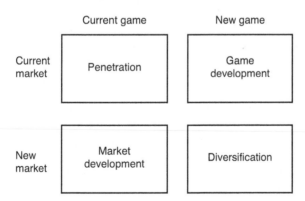

Figure 3.4 Product/market expansion grid

Source: Ansoff, 1957, p. 114

A *market development* strategy means that you are convinced that your game is a great game, but you are not targeting the right market. The consumers that you initially thought would appreciate the game and buy it pay no or little attention to the game. The result is that you need to take this game to another market, to another segment of consumers. If you have done an analysis of the market potential of the game when developing it, you should have identified a number of different segments of consumers who might find your game interesting. In this case you need to go back to your analysis and see what alternative segments it would be possible to attract. It might also be the case that your game is gaining attention and market share in a market other than your target market. This again indicates that your target market is not where you should focus. A marketing development strategy is thus about taking your current game to a new market.

A *diversification* strategy involves taking a new game to a new market. This might be the strategy that has the largest risk, because having both a new game and a new market suggests that there are many unknown factors involved. Too many unknown factors will make it harder for you to formulate a strategy based on your knowledge of games and different potential markets. When you are developing your first game or games, this will be the situation you are in – low experience of the game and low experience of the market. A diversification strategy may bring you back to this position, but it can also help you to find new markets that you previously were not aware of. The reason for pursuing a diversification strategy can be that your game is not doing well on the present market, but you see great potential taking this game to another market if you change the game somewhat.

The different strategies outlined in this chapter can also be applied as part of your game portfolio management. All of your games taken together might be published for a very specific market. If that market decreases, there is a need to change the profile of the game portfolio. Electronic Arts uses a strategy that requires that they limit risk by publishing games for different markets. They are putting their eggs in different baskets, so to speak. In Chapter 4 we talk about brands in the game industry. The learning point here is that having strong brand recognition can mean that you have a greater possibility for diversification. When consumers know your brand, they may trust you enough to buy games that they normally would not buy, just because you have developed them.

Exercises

1   Re-imagine your game in terms of service and experience. What type of new insights does this new perspective bring to your project? Can you identify new competitors you haven't thought off previously – maybe competitors that are not even in the game industry?

2   Analyze your favourite game according to the three layers of game experience as described in this chapter.

3   Apply the repositioning-of-game-experiences framework to your own game development project. Is there a need for a repositioning? Can your game project benefit from a repositioning?

4   Brands and video games

In this chapter we discuss the basics of branding. We start with one of the most basic functions of branding – to represent values based on associations. If your actions are successful, they will produce a situation where consumers will think of your brand when they think of your product/service category (think of a soft drink and we guarantee you that you were thinking of Coca-Cola). To help you understand how branding can work on a more complex level, we introduce concepts from brand architecture that are useful when working with multiple brands from one company – which is very much the case with the game industry, where many game titles become brands of their own. In order to handle multiple brands, we need brand positioning, which is a tool to create brand strategies. Finally, we need to understand various concepts from the field of brand management that aim to manage brands to become successful and profitable.

Learning objectives

1   To recognize what a brand means in relation to products and services and in a game industry setting
2   To understand basic branding concepts such as brand associations, architecture, positioning and top-of-mind brand recognition
3   To understand how brand management can be useful for game development

Introduction

Who doesn't recognize the brands Mario, Sonic, Grand Theft Auto, Call of Duty, Battlefield, Angry Birds, Electronic Arts, Blizzard, Vivendi and Nintendo? These are not so much specific video game titles, developers or publishers but more a wide-ranging set of stories, memories, impressions, feelings and experiences that are tied together by the notion of a "brand". They find their way into the minds of hundreds of millions of us consumers – and stay there, influencing our perception, emotions and purchasing behaviour toward video games. This is an incredibly powerful tool that not only exists in the repertoire of inspirational speakers and business pundits but is tangibly present in the shape of billion-dollar valuations on balance sheets of some of the biggest names in the industry. Slightly threadbare in its valuation methodology, Forbes estimates that the Apple brand is alone worth more than *120 billion USD*, which is in the same range as the nominal total gross domestic product of Hungary, a dynamically evolving EU member with almost 10 million inhabitants. Although we shouldn't put too much faith into these valuations – after all, Apple can't sell its brand without destroying it – it definitely puts the effect of branding into perspective.

Companies like Apple and Nike highlight the fact that we are living in a branded society. The importance of brands can be seen everywhere. If you want, you can try counting the number of brands you are exposed to each day on your way to work or school – it will be thousands! So, obviously, brands mean something to us. Many of us also participate in different *brand tribes*: communities dedicated to specific brands, whether Harley Davidson, Apple, Nintendo or any other brand that engages us. This has been picked up from companies that are creating business ideas around strong brands. It is not farfetched to claim that Nike and, in many aspects, Apple are brand companies. Their main focus is to construct strong brands that will enable them to both gain large market shares and charge premium price for their products. As long as the performance of their products matches or exceeds what is promised through brand communication, it works. Although these are examples of extreme focus on brands, something that we have not seen in the games industry yet, they highlight the impact brands have on business, cultures and society.

Brands represent all the aspects of what games and game companies mean to different people; this means that the brand(s) of a company are among its most valuable properties. Primarily this means that gamers recognize and incorporate the meaning of brands in their relationships with games and companies. Therefore it makes good sense to construct strong brands and nurture these to play a big role for gamers in their relationships to games and game developers. All the work we described in the previous chapter about positioning your company and games should be materialized in your brand – the values and ambitions that have gone into planning where your company is going and how it should be materialized into a brand that will have the capability of taking you there, wherever you are going.

Top of the mind!

Having a strong brand serves the purpose of ensuring that your company is present in the decision-making process of consumers when they are choosing what games to buy – or any other product, for that matter. That is, branding can make your company top of the mind for gamers that you are aiming at. This means that the brand will always be part of whatever alternative consumers are thinking about. Think the position of Apple computers. No matter whether you like Apple or not, it has reached a position where it is top of the mind for many consumers. The effect is that when these consumers think about buying a new computer, they exclude most brands when evaluating alternatives. The question that is asked is not "What new computer do I buy?" but "What new Mac do I buy?"

For the games industry, this specifically means that gamers are more likely to buy games because of the brand, because they assume that the name of the game or developer communicates something desirable for them. This means buying the new Need for Speed because the prequels were good games or buying new games from Blizzard because they appreciated playing World of Warcraft.

Power of associations

Brands work because they mean something to us, or, to be more precise, they work *if* they mean something to us. A successful brand is therefore dependent on the values that are inscribed into the brand, something that has to come from the company but at the same time is agreed to and supported by consumers. And, if you think about it, brands never mean anything per se – every meaning has been created intentionally. All of these aspects taken together create a brand identity: consumer experience, marketing communication, activities, people, stories, images, culture and meaning. A graphical image without these aspects is just a sign (see Figure 4.1).

Think about the well-known brands that we are surrounded by. A good example is Jack Daniels, a whiskey that is sold in a signature square bottle. This brand has been the target for an intention and successful brand strategy. Looking at what that product actually is – well, it is a brownish liquid. It has a specific taste, similar to the taste of what we define as whiskey. It also contains alcohol, which has certain effects on your body when you drink it. But aside from that, nothing more! If you talk to people about Jack Daniels, most will give you an image of a whiskey that is as much about sex, drugs and rock n' roll as it is about whiskey. This is, of course, an image that the Jack Daniels company has worked very hard to establish. This includes stories about Jack, celebrity endorsements from people who embody these symbols (Slash from Guns 'n' Roses) and communications whose images and text build the same

Figure 4.1 Symbol – brand identity

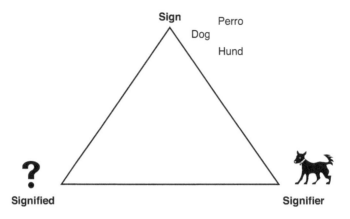

Figure 4.2 Sign: signifier – signified

Source: Saussure, 1916/1995

image. But there is nothing inherent in Jack Daniels that is sex, drugs and rock 'n' roll.

In the games industry we can see something similar in the position Electronic Arts has created. Unlike Jack Daniels, the games that come out of EA Sports in Vancouver already have a symbolical value – in this case, sports. What EA is doing, though, is to strengthen these sports values, both physically in the Vancouver campus and also in text and images that are communicated about EA Sports. Unlike the example of Jack Daniels, EA Sport is all about sports. The values embraced in sports thus strengthen the EA brands, through marketing activities. Or we can take other examples, such as Rockstar Games, which develops the Grand Theft Auto games. It is the bad boy of the game industry, both in product and in market communication. Bad press about Rockstar might even strengthen its image as the bad boy of the industry.

This is where the power of associations comes into play. A brand can be loaded with different values. In order to create a strong brand, it is necessary to transfer the values from the company or the game to the brand in order to create a strong brand identity, a coherent way in which consumers understand a brand. A way of thinking about this is that all signs have two different sides: what it signifies and what is signified (see Figure 4.2). Think about the word "dog", for example. This is a sign. In other languages there are other signs with the same meaning: *hund, perro, chien* and so on. All of these signs point toward that furry animal with four legs. That is the signifier of the sign. But, what is signified by "dog" is not clear. Depending on whom you ask, it can mean different things: a cuddly friend, a guard of your property, a companion for hunting or a terrifying beast with big fangs that attacks on sight. When it comes to brands, you have to make sure that everyone understands your brand the same way.

Brand architecture

Not all brands are the same. There are many times different types of brands, even within the same company; each brand functions to communicate the meaning of a specific company, product or series of products. There is much sense in branding different parts of the company, but they all need to support the mission of the company in order to build coherent and strong communication with consumers.

Company brand is the name of the company and the values it represents, for example Activision, Rockstar or Blizzard Entertainment. There can also be different companies in the same organization, meaning that there are different brands that have to collaborate and, if possible, strengthen the values they represent.

Product brand is a product or line of products developed by a company, for example Call of Duty or Need for Speed. Overall they represent the values of the organization, but the products might have different focuses, as they are developed to attract different markets. When starting a company developing games, entrepreneurs often make the mistake of using the same brand name for both company and game. This is a result of a strong focus on the game; it might also be the only reason for starting that company! But keep in mind that when the company grows, it should be more than that first game.

Character brand is the features that are used in games to enhance gaming recognition, such as including a character that has been featured in a long string of games or a character from a film or a historical person. The reason these brands are so successful is that consumers have parasocial relationships with these characters. It is almost as if we know them, as part of our social circle of friends. The value of these brands has created a market where these are traded as intellectual properties (IP).

Employer brand is communicated not only to consumers but also to potential co-workers and collaborators, to future programmers, graphical artists and other persons the industry needs. These brands communicate the culture of working and collaborating with this company. A good example is Google, which has managed to create a very successful employer brand. This has resulted in Google being ranked in 2015 as the most attractive employer. Having a strong employer brand makes it possible to attract persons who are highly competent and also support the culture of your company. This is important, as culture is not something you can build in a company; culture is the result of the people working there.

Fighter brand is a brand that is launched but initially not associated with the company brand or other product brands in the company. This gives a company the possibility to try out a new product or line of products without any negative backlashes if the product fails. When building value through creating a strong brand identity, there are possibilities of brand extensions (more about this later). But, as there are limits to how far a brand can be stretched and still keep its value, fighter brands offer opportunities to try out new markets without damaging other brands in the company.

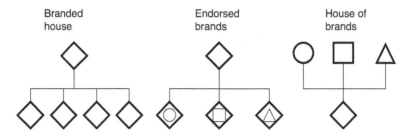

Figure 4.3 Brand relationship spectrum

It is important that a company choose what brand(s) to promote in its market communication. Different brands can also be communicated in different ways or in different settings. For example do gamers buy games because of the developer, publisher or game title? Depending on the answer to this question, one will communicate different brands at different times. Building a strong company brand will benefit all product brands that are associated with the company, but for consumers it might make more sense to communicate the game brands.

It might be the case that your consumers do not care about your company brand. And why should they, if they are interested only in your games? In other industries the manufacturer and headquarters are rarely communicated by a company's products. There are, for example, few that notice the company name Procter & Gamble. But we all know the products in the P&G family: Ariel, Braun, Head & Shoulders, Pampers, Tampax.

If there are several brands in your company, there needs to be a clear relationship between them, whether you are creating games that are part of the same brand or releasing games that are part of separate brands. The brand relationship spectrum in figure 4.3 shows different possible relationships between different brands: corporate brand, branded house, endorsed brands/sub-brands and house of brands.

The corporate brand (or umbrella or family brand) is the name of the "parent brand" in the diagram in the figure. The corporate brand represents the company behind multiple brands, and the relationship to the parent brand may differ according to the setup.

A branded house is one in which the corporate brand covers all the brands of the house. The brand is in a monolithic and dominating position over its range of products/services. A typical example might be the skin care brand Dove, which sells everything from soap to shower creams, lotions, deodorants and hair care products – but the Dove brand looms above every product and there is no separation of the different product lines as separate brands.

Endorsed brands or sub-brands are those that are organized under a parent brand, and the parent adds credibility and strength to the brand. For instance Sony PlayStation is the typical endorsed brand; the PlayStation brand is endorsed by the strength of the Sony brand and its image. PlayStation has become independent to a certain degree and in many situations it acts as such – but in formative marketing communications the parent brand is always present.

A house of brands is one in which the individual brands of the house exist on their own without the symbolic interference of their house brand. This is the case for most FMCG (Fast-Moving Consumer Goods – that is, most products sold in grocery stores). Although many consumers recognize the independent brands of the razor brand Gillette, the diaper brand Pampers and the battery brand Duracell, the corporate brand of all of these brands, Procter & Gamble, is not displayed in these brands' marketing communications.

All of these brand architecture strategies are highly relevant in the game industry, where various game companies have chosen different strategies depending on their history, product portfolio and other factors.

Brand positioning and anatomy

In order to create a strong brand that has the possibility of becoming top of the mind, it is important to have a clear and comprehensive strategy. This strategy, just like any other strategy, is important when the brand is initially created. But

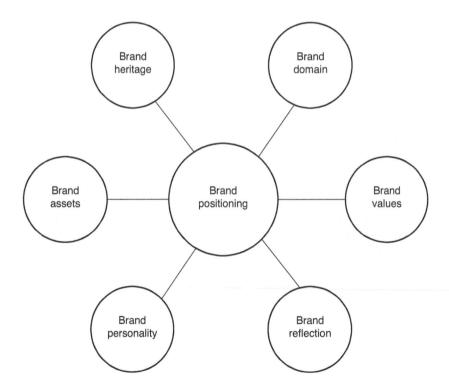

Figure 4.4 Brand anatomy of brand positioning

it is equally important that the strategy be iterative and something that is revised when the environment changes.

The strength of a brand is built upon six different elements that together form the brand's anatomy: brand domain, brand heritage, brand value, brand assets, brand personality and brand reflections. The *brand domain* is the target market for the brand. In order for a strong brand to be communicated, it is important that you know your audience. How else would you know how to address it? In Chapter 1 we described the segmentation that needs to be in place in any marketing strategy. A brand is thus a result of the choices made in that plan. Just as in any other setting, it is close to impossible to speak to everyone all the time and stay interesting.

Brand heritage is the background of the brand, how it became successful and its development. Here are where the stories are important, stories that build the history of the brand. We all love the story about how Markus "Notch" Persson created Minecraft (Mojang) as a side project while working another day job. This story creates the legend of the game and the company. It enables us all to dream of that tiny chance that if we build it, they will come. No matter how insignificant it may seem, most successful brands have a creation myth. No history account of Apple is complete without mentioning the garage where the founders created the beginning of a strong brand; Microsoft's history stories always includes how Bill Gates dropped out of Harvard University because he didn't want to miss the opportunity to build his vision of software technology.

Brand value reflects the value of the company or its products. The values of Grand Theft Auto (Rockstar Games) are different from those of Unravel (Electronic Arts), for example. Although they are both games, they communicate different modes and emotions – and, in the end, a consumer should expect different things when playing these two games. The brand values are those that the brand/company identifies *itself* with – the values that the company has chosen as constituting its core identity. As with any other type of communal identity values, these brand values are rarely negative – nobody wants to identify with a brand that openly professes negative values. Even those that could be considered negative (e.g. non-ethical, non-ecological, non-humane) by many will somehow emphasize their relative best side (e.g. "Of all the oil companies in the world we invest the most in renewable energy research"). In other words, the values of your game brand must be prudently analyzed and well considered because they represent more than merely what you as a brand *want* to be – these values have to be anchored in the real-life dimensions of the brand.

Brand assets are the unique qualities that differentiate your brand from other brands. For games these are the unique features that differentiate your game from those of your competitors. This can be an engine that renders the graphics realistic over multiplayer modes and other features. It is important that these features be something that the consumer defines as unique and that he or she can appreciate. This is based on a fundamental assumption of marketing management that states that unique and distinctive features of a brand will always produce *valuable* assets, which in a market economy is the equivalent of increased sales. Most brands emphasize unique properties in order to position themselves in a corner of the market that they "own". Nintendo's Super Mario brand "owns" the market for Super Mario – since most similar games are simply imitations. Yet, in the end it must be a uniqueness that consumers/target audiences *recognize* – while Nintendo might consider Super Mario unique, the marketplace might, after a while, merely consider it yet another platform game brand. Therefore it is important that the uniqueness of the brand asset be one that is identified not only by the brand/company but *also* by the consumers.

Brand personality is also sometimes known as brand identity and essentially means those human characteristics that are associated with a brand. Within this model it definitely represents a turn in our consumer society toward a more personal perspective on branding. In contemporary society, brands have become more than symbols representing the attributes of companies and their products and have instead become symbols that are incorporated into the lifestyles, identities and values of modern consumers. As modern consumers, we build relationships based on our own experience/history with the brand pre- and post-purchase, the opinions of other people/consumers and the marketing communication of the brand. For instance many Apple consumers own a dozen Apple products; they interact daily for hours during work as well as leisure time with Apple products; they gladly put Apple logo stickers on their cars and follow live streams of Apple product launches. Apple stores have become tourist attractions for travellers. Obviously brands have become considerably more personal, and therefore it is more natural that they take on personality-like traits in our associations.

Brand reflections are the final step and decide how a brand's heritage, values, assets and personality are incorporated by the consumers after they purchase and use the brand's products. This is a dimension that has historically been overlooked by much of marketing management and by marketing industry practice – many marketing strategies have overemphasized the importance of completing the purchasing decision/transaction, sometimes at the cost of damaging the brand's long-term reputation (e.g. brands that don't deliver on their various promises, possibly creating a deterioration of brand assets). Post-purchase branding is not merely limited to good customer service but involves at a strategic level a general consistency in the brand anatomy. A brand that continuously modifies its brand anatomy alienates existing consumers and may even create conflicts between "old" and "new" target audiences. Therefore it is important to consider the entire brand and how it fits into the reflections of its consumers.

Brand management

Brand management is the discipline of managing brands from a corporate/company perspective. There is plenty of research as well as ample practice to learn from. First of all, in this perspective, it is important to understand the difference between brand and intellectual property (IP). "Brand" is a term that has no legal dimension but is mainly a marketing and symbolic term. Super Mario is a brand since it represents all the video games in the Super Mario series. It also represents the Mario character, and the brand also represents thousands of associations created during the years by its owner, Nintendo, and the millions of consumers who have interacted with this brand. It is also a copyrighted and *legal* trademark that nobody except Nintendo has the right to use commercially. Not *every* single character or object in the Super Mario games is a registered trademark, but they may also, in terms of marketing communications, have the properties of a brand since consumers identify them with Super Mario and other associations. Therefore it is important within brand management to decide what dimensions/aspects of your game can be trademarked and potentially turned into separate commercial products/service brands or whether merely the title of the game is the main trademark.

Let us briefly walk through the major concepts within brand management and discuss how they can be applied within your game development project: brand identity/values, awareness, image, engagement/loyalty, extensions and equity.

Brand identity/values are the identifying values that the company behind the brand considers the core characteristics and associations that constitute the brand. These values are the ones the company aims to communicate to consumers as accurately and as precisely as possible in order for the consumers to share these values and associations. In other words it constitutes the company's *aspiration* regarding the brand. Usually this involves all the (visual) marketing

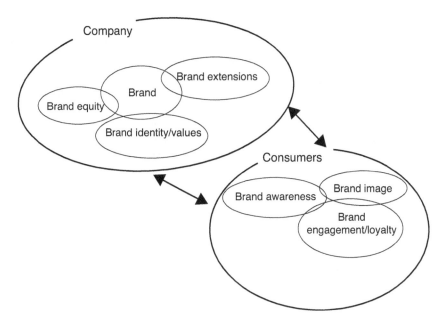

Figure 4.5 Brand strategy process

communications that (physically) manifest these values from the company, for instance the logotype, graphical profile, advertising, PR, website and any other resource managed by the company that will be exposed to the consumer.

Brand awareness is the recognition of the brand among consumers. This was discussed previously as "top of mind" and refers to the brand that most consumers associate with a product without any cues or help. If you ask someone to name the number one smartphone brand, the most likely answer is the iPhone brand. When their response is triggered by the question "Which of the following brands are smartphone manufacturers? 1. Apple 2. Samsung 3. Marshall?," consumers will be as aware of the Apple brand as of the Samsung brand, and Marshall (also a smartphone brand!) would probably have very low recognition.

Brand image is the identity of the brand as perceived by *consumers*. As we show in Chapter 5, marketing communications do not work like brainwashing propaganda; not everything stated by the company/brand is perceived and remembered in the same way by all consumers. Instead, a vast majority of consumers are constantly being bombarded with numerous branding efforts on a daily basis, and most consumers actively resist branding and marketing communications by ignoring them, switching the channel or closing down the pop-up or app. Nonetheless, the aim of brand management is in essence to minimize the gap between the brand identity and the brand image. This can be achieved by (costly) brute force, for example by buying so much advertising space that consumers most likely *cannot* escape the message. Or the company can switch strategies and try to appeal to consumers so that they will actively search for that brand and regard the advertising with interest.

Brand engagement/loyalty is the personal relationship consumers have with the brand and, by extension, their loyalty toward the brand. Brand engagement is possible *prior* to purchase of the product – people queueing for hours (or days!) before the launch of the latest smartphone or game already show signs of great brand engagement without yet having engaged with the product. Post-purchase brand engagement can assume many forms, but one of the most important, from the company's point of view, is brand loyalty, expressed as repeated purchases of the same brand, since repeat customers are substantially more profitable than new consumers, whose acquisition costs decrease considerably the general profit margin.

Brand extensions involve combining, extending and cross-breeding brands. A game-related (but ultimately failed) case of brand extension is Microsoft's decision to extend the Xbox brand to digital music streaming. The logic behind brand extension is to capitalize on brand awareness and recognition that the brand has previously built up in another market and to use it in a new and "extended" marketplace. The nature of the extension dictates the success – somehow consumers or Microsoft concluded that Xbox and music did not go well together, despite the initial assumption that the strong brand recognition of Xbox in digital entertainment would lend itself to a digital music streaming service.

So-called *brand equity* constitutes the core of the brand management perspective – the ability or wish to create measurable financial results, visible on balance sheets for shareholders, as a result of brand management strategies and activities – in other words, adapting and aligning marketing, branding and communication activities with a ROI (return on investment) perspective. The origin of this perspective is the need to measure in financial terms the value of a company's brand(s), since brands are not included as resources on balance sheets from a strictly accounting point of view (except roughly as goodwill when buying or merging with another company). In cases of publicly listed consumer-goods companies such as Nike, this poses a slight financial problem since most of the company's production line is outsourced to various low-wage countries, and practically all of its stock valuation is locked inside the value of the brand, where fairly unmeasurable dimensions such as brand, design, brand identity and many others ultimately decide the financial value. Brand equity is an attempt, using various methods and calculations, to standardize the objective valuation of various brand dimensions to prove the financial value of the brand.

Exercises

1   Take five top-of-mind brands that come to your mind from different game-related products and services, and discuss why you think these brands have achieved this elevated position.

2   Analyze two major game brands, such as game console brands, in terms of their brand architecture. Can you see any differences in their approach? Why is that the case?

3   Use the tools presented in this chapter related to brand management and apply these to your game development project. What kind of insight have you gained? How do you make your brand successful in the crowded marketplace?

5 Marketing communications and video games

This chapter is about marketing communications, which are an essential part of the marketing process. Our definition of marketing communications is based on a deeper explanation of what marketing, communications and consumers signify in this context. We present several categorizations of marketing communications – the first is bought/paid, earned/non-paid and owned media communications, while the second framework builds on models of one-way and two-way communications. The categorizations are used to explain the traditional type of marketing communications such as advertising, PR/strategic communications and marketing communications. The chapter concludes by discussing new perspectives that can cross the boundaries of these established categorizations of marketing communications.

Learning objectives

1 To learn what marketing communications includes and how it is part of marketing
2 To recognize different types and categories of marketing communications
3 To learn the differences among marketing communications, advertising and PR
4 To recognize how marketing communications can be applied to video games marketing

Introduction

Marketing communications is the area of marketing most people are exposed to on a daily basis: different companies trying to communicate with us with marketing messages about what to wear, what cars to buy or what games to play. We live in a constant torrent of messages: billboards, advertisements, pop-ups, Facebook advertising, to mention a few. Our being so used to the clutter of messages presents challenges for developers trying to break through this "noise" of competing messages. But there is strong evidence that suggests that successful marketing communications have the possibility to support sustainable businesses by creating relationships with consumers through (marketing) communication processes.

It is important to point out at the beginning of this chapter something rather obvious. When talking about marketing communications we do mean "communications", not a marketing monologue. This one-too-many communication mode has long since played out its role and is considered outdated by both industry and research. No one is interested in listening only – we want to participate in a dialogue. Therefore any marketing communications have to incorporate the consumers, the persons you are talking to, in the process. In that sense, you must move to a many-to-many communication where your company is only one of the participants.

In the beginning of this book we wrote that many of you might think of advertising when you think of marketing. "Let us market what this game means" – usually through advertising. That seems natural, since all the marketing communications that we are exposed to daily are part of various marketing processes. But, as we have seen throughout this book, marketing starts much earlier. We would argue that game marketing that starts with a finished or nearly finished product has a high risk of failing in the marketplace. The problem is this: how can you communicate something to anyone without knowing to whom you are talking, what you are talking about and how you should talk about it? We suggest that marketing communications that incorporate what has been discussed so far in the book, that is, an inclusive and more extensive approach to marketing, have a much higher chance of being successful!

In the video game industry there are a number of challenges when it comes to marketing communications. We believe that some of these are generic problems that you would meet in any industry, while others are unique to this industry. There are two main challenges that we see, the first one generic and the second one specific. The generic problem is the vast number of games being released on a daily basis – how do you break through and compete with that? The second unique problem is that many of the marketing communications of games are out of the developers' hands and dependent on the whims of the publisher and/or the platform owner.

By building a strategy for marketing communications, based on a solid marketing plan, you have the possibility to create a more cohesive communication that connects with every relevant partner – publishers, distributors, platform owners, game media, game conferences, developer community and various segments of game consumers.

What is marketing communications?

Marketing

What marketing means is, we hope, clearer to you after five chapters of this book. Instead of repeating what has been already said, we want to emphasize some important aspects in a context of communication. Marketing is created by institutions and processes for communicating with customers, clients, partners and society at large. What's more, marketing communications *can* involve promotion, advertising and sales but do not comprise only these activities commonly understood as equivalents to marketing (communications).

Another important issue is: why market*ing* communications and not market communications? Simply put, the answer is that the concept of market communications involves activities in a market and must be dependent on clear-cut definitions of markets and whether or not these communication activities can be considered part of the market. Market*ing* communications bypasses this discussion by focusing on the process and intent of the communication – if the communication is done with the intent to aid the marketing of goods and services, then it is classified as marketing communications. By this more process-oriented perspective, a government agency can use marketing communications tools and strategies (such as branding, targeted communication campaigns, target group segmentation and advertising) without having to define whether or not "it's in a market" – if the intent is to communicate their goods and services as existing in a market, then *it is* marketing communication. If the very same government agency in a different setting uses a completely different mode of communication that does not relate to the market(s) – let us say, official announcements – then it is no longer using marketing communications but instead doing public information work. Intent is of course sometimes very difficult, if not impossible, to determine – but it is significantly easier to determine the type of marketing tools, strategies and concepts present in the communication strategies of various organizations. If a public unemployment agency communicates to unemployed workers as "clients" or "customers" in relation to "job markets" and "targets" potential employers as "market segments" and is using advertising space in commercial media channels, then this can be considered marketing communications even though the public agency has a state-funded monopoly and is not profit driven.

Marketing communications apply a company/brand/organization focus to the marketing process. There are alternative perspectives within the broad category of marketing communications that focus on consumers or the medium itself (media planning and search engine optimization, to mention two), but in this book we focus primarily on a specific company – a video game developer – that wants to communicate a marketing message about its new video game title. Therefore, we present perspectives that assume that the company/brand perspectives are the most important ones, although intricate knowledge of the consumer's perspectives is increasingly becoming a strategic advantage for branding/marketing communications as a whole.

The dominant marketing management tradition since the 1960s states that a marketing strategy is based on the marketing mix of the 4Ps – product, price, place and promotion – which we have discussed in previous chapters. Marketing communications are in this perspective constituted by the last P; it has for decades been delegated a promotional function that extends the remaining three Ps by instructing, informing and selling through mass-media communication channels. In other words, the role of marketing communications in traditional marketing strategy is to inform as many consumers as possible, through the mass media, of the existence of a certain product, at a certain store or reseller, at a certain (attractive) price.

Communications

Communication is one of those complicated notions that are behind much of human civilization since it is hard to imagine something or someone who does *not* communicate to us humans. Tea leaves communicate about the future; the smile of the Mona Lisa communicates secrets that still intrigue us centuries after anyone involved in its making have gone. Spoken-word communication makes usually the most sense – but not always. Music can communicate the most intense emotions – but what does it really *mean*?

The word "communication" derives from the original Latin *communicare*, meaning "to share" – thus, communicating is about sharing something. This is an extremely broad definition, but in this book we turn our attention to the actual processes of communicating and the forms they assume. Even more to the point, these communication forms have, during the past two centuries, evolved into *tele*-communications (communication over long distances), which gave rise to *media* communications and, later, *mass* communications (when media reached the majority of a population). Media, with an immensely broad definition, are an inescapable part of today's society. A short explanation comes from the Latin origin of *medium*, meaning "a means of conveying something". In other words, media can bridge and connect two points, which suits the "sharing" meaning of communication – something is shared by two (or more parties) and something must bridge them in order for the sharing to happen. This bridge has in modern society become technology, which drives its form, possibilities and, to some extent, content.

It is impossible to understand modern marketing communications without media communications. Actually the original and still most dominating objective of marketing communications is exposure in (mass) media, usually through advertising (which we discuss later). Promotion/publicity/advertising, public relations, media relations, press agentry and public information – that's all what marketing communications should do, right? This chapter explains that there are definitely more forward-looking perspectives on what modern marketing communications are all about.

There is a traditional perspective on communications and also a more contemporary one. The traditional one can be summarized as a *transmission-based* view of communication in which a *sender* formulates a message to be communicated and converts this message into a *channel* or *medium*, which then reaches the *receiver*. Although created for telecommunication technologies, the model has had tremendous success in formulating our understanding of the mass media, since it corresponds quite well with the author-text-reader perspectives of literary theory: the author creates a message and turns it into a text, and then a reader reads it. This linear process, focused on codifying (creating) messages and decodifying (receiving) them, corresponds to expressing a message and then later interpreting it. If the message is decodified or interpreted "the wrong way" in relation to the encoding, according to the sender, then, in line with the transmission perspective, "noise" has disturbed the communication process. Noise simply means deviating interpretations by audiences. This "noise perspective" is one in which the formulation of the sender or author is considered superior, and the interpretations of receiver or reader are considered optimal when they agree with the sender's view and erroneous "noise" otherwise. Despite this somewhat hierarchical and unfavourable attitude toward the receiver/reader/audience, it is still a dominating view in much of media and marketing communications. The marketing communications function of a brand, according to many, is to convey a message to consumers with as little noise as possible, that is, to lecture and instruct consumers about the message, and if there is too much noise (the message doesn't get through as intended), the strategy of the brand/sender is to reformulate its message and strategy until the consumers/audiences/receivers are interpreting the message the way the sender intends. As you might understand, this is not a very sustainable perspective since in some ways it approaches communication as a friendly type of propaganda.

Although not intended to be partial toward one-way-communication from sender to receiver, the traditional perspective did indeed encourage a concentration of efforts on the sender/author and the medium/text, since the development of the mass media gave rise to a media age of one-to-many communication where a tiny elite of journalists and officials in massive media houses using extremely expensive technological tools created media content for the masses. In a marketing communications setting, this was also highly relevant; companies and brands wanted to promote their messages to as many potential buyers as possible. Therefore, marketing communications were and still are dominated by perspectives that discuss *what, how* and *when* (message formulation) to say something as a marketer, *where* to say it (which channel or medium) and to *whom* (a limited audience) except when using very broad categorizations such as "women, between the age of eighteen and thirty-four, in need of cars/transportation". In other words, marketing communications have evolved together with the growth of the mass media.

All of this has of course radically changed during the past few decades. After decades (centuries in some media cases) mass communication is no longer one-to-many but has transformed into many-to-many communications. This has been dictated not by technological innovation only (digitalization, Internet, smartphones), but primarily by societal and cultural change. Since the 1960s audiences in Western societies and in many other parts of the world have objected to their passive role as receivers of hierarchical communication – they want to express their own individual meaning and opinion and participate more actively in societal discussions. The contemporary age of communication enabled by the technological revolution of digitalization and the Internet can be summarized in the "selfie" – a picture you take of yourself and post on social media networks for your (sometimes millions of) followers who have chosen to receive your communication – but also expect to interact with that content (likes, comments, sharing and forwarding) and who have the exact same possibilities to communicate in the same way. Mass communication has turned to the individual – the readers/receivers/audiences/consumers have grown up and have (on paper) the same marketing communications tools at their disposal as the long-established media houses and their elites such as journalists, politicians and brands. The new communication era is based on dialogue, interpretation and two-way communication. These have revolutionized marketing communications since they are elemental parts of the media communications landscape of most democratic market economy–based societies.

Consumers

Companies and brands have changed remarkably during the transformation of media and marketing communications – but one fundamental property remains unaffected, and that is the need to reach as many consumers as possible. This need is, has always been, and will always be fundamental to all marketing communications. The other essential partner – the consumers/audience/receivers – has also radically changed, except that they keep on consuming. Everything about consumers and consumption has radically evolved during the transformation of marketing, societies and cultures.

As with communications perspectives, there is a traditional perspective on these changes and also a more contemporary one. In the traditional view consumers are seen as passive receivers of marketing communications messages created by companies and brands. The consumer is the objective and starting point of the marketing-oriented business – according to traditional marketing communications theory, successful communication starts with the needs of the consumer and, after careful and strategic formulation of the message by the company, ends with a message received by the consumer. The needs of the consumer can and should be interpreted by the company *before* the product is even designed. Know your audience – do not create a video game only for yourself or for your like-minded developer community; create it for a greater audience and their gaming needs. Marketing communications also teaches us not to analyze only customers' gaming needs but also their communication needs – a certain target audience might love your game idea but not buy it because the marketing communications are not adapted to their specific sensibilities.

The consumer in the traditional marketing communications perspective is an autonomous subject, an individual who takes independent purchasing decisions, and the aggregate decisions of similar people constitute a target audience. A consumer is related to other consumers by means of so-called reference groups that affect the consumer's purchasing decisions. Therefore, traditional marketing communications theory recommends appealing to the individual consumer in the first place and also, from a company or brand perspective, to his or her reference groups, that is, groups against which individuals compare themselves.

Let us say that your video game appeals to the hardcore gamer target group; your game will have to adapt to the needs of this group, but it also needs to take into account the needs of the individual consumer. Despite identifying with a collective, people have plenty of individual preferences and needs that you also need to account for when creating your marketing communications strategy.

Finally, traditional marketing communications are heavily focused on the actual transaction – the decision by the consumer to buy a product or service. A lot of theories in the 1950s and since focused on the decision theory of purchasing choices, on the assumption that consumers tend to make rational decisions that are the best possible after considering the available information. In other words, faced with two products with equivalent user value, the consumer will buy the cheaper option. As a result, much of traditional marketing communications theory focuses on communicating pricing, availability, features, resellers and discounts in order to smooth the purchasing transaction. Later research argued that a broader perspective beyond the narrow purchasing decisions must be adopted in order to fully understand consumer behaviour.

Contemporary perspectives set aside the strictly hierarchical, monodirectional "noise-reducing" company- or brand-centric purchasing transaction–focused perspectives and embrace a two-way marketing communication perspective. In this modern perspective, consumers actively interpret the symbols of their surroundings, including brand, other consumers and their consumption and their own relational history, to products that affect relations to particular brands and products. Marketing communications are happening everywhere and should not merely focus on the company's desire to increase sales of the company/brand but should instead embrace the communication process.

Brand or company is merely one of many "authors" of the communications surrounding the brand – most marketing communications happen *outside* the control, influence and authorship of companies and brands. Marketing communications are everywhere – when a friend is wearing a jacket with a certain brand, when we see someone unknown on the bus carrying a bag of the same brand, when we see a famous person on social media wearing the brand in his or her personal life, when someone we dislike wears the brand (football hooligans wearing Lonsdale sweaters), when we discover that people talk about a brand in positive or negative ways (e.g. "Burberry is the brand of chavs"; "Land Rover is the timeless brand of the understated British upper class"), when we finally buy the product on sale in an unpleasant outlet or are convinced to try a new brand by a very charming salesperson, when the product is broken and we encounter good or bad customer service, when we buy the product because we associate it with family memories (e.g. "My father always liked Omega watches, and my grandmother once made a huge impression on me as a child when she wore Chanel No. 5"), when we associate products with ethnicity and national culture (e.g. "Swedes love their Volvos because they're slightly reserved, appreciate quality and technology, dislike gaudy luxury and value safety"), or when we relate to a brand in relation to our personal values (e.g. "I want to be eco-friendly, but the only way to organize my family's life is to own a car, and VW offers diesel cars with very low emissions" – and then it turns out the emissions were tampered with), and so on. All of these voices are indeed affected by the company or brand and in many ways the company does constitute the loudest voice in a marketing communications context. But it is a one-sided misconstruction to ignore all these other voices or to believe that they can all be managed with efficient marketing management.

Contemporary perspectives reverse the traditional view that marketing is about consumers being independent from marketing and consumer society. In this perspective, the consumers *become* the product of the consumer society and its marketing strategies. Society is not the aggregated result of consumers' decisions; it is the other way around, where the consumer is the result of social relations with other consumers, subculture, brands and the market. In contemporary society the consumer defines his or her identity through shopping and cannot choose not to consume. Being "anti-consumption", perhaps by wearing vintage clothing, living without social media, and sending SMS messages with a fifteen-year-old Nokia mobile phone, is *also* a consumption lifestyle. Consumption in large part defines what we are. Want to leave the busy city for the quiet countryside and live as ecologically as possible? There is no escaping the marketing communication industries and their strategies. These consumer lifestyles are actively targeted by makers of ecologically safe products in practically every category (even cars, entire houses and airlines) – brands with "eco-consciousness", locally sourced and produced goods, "upcycling" and so on.

If we relate this to video game markets, we find there are hardcore, casual, mainstream and countless other type of gamers with different lifestyles, needs, preferences and sensibilities. But the traditional marketing way of surveying reference groups and then creating an abstract demographical target audience profile to reach is, with a modern perspective, not necessarily the best approach. With a contemporary marketing communications approach, there must be an understanding that video games become part of a game culture and that new titles, marketing communications and marketing activities are not speaking *to* the culture, they *are* part of that culture, and every marketing communication message, game or activity is a contribution that interacts and affects this game culture. Therefore a modern marketing communications strategy considers the video game and its communication in a bigger cultural context, where a game developer is not someone who merely creates games but is someone who participates actively in the gaming community – not invisibly through niched developer forums or by reactively during some type of crisis situation but actively in dialogue with audiences.

Consumers are real human social beings and not, as traditional marketing would have it, receivers of a static message. Consumers relate to and interpret *everything* in social terms – themselves, other consumers, products and services, speech and attitudes about certain brands and products, advertising and so on – and *all* of these affect how marketing communication works, as well as consumer attitudes toward brands and consumer purchasing decisions. It is impossible to isolate the consumer as an autonomous subject, since almost all forms of consumption are social – even gaming alone involves a need to share the experience later, whether through high scores on various Web forums or social network-like multiplayer networks such as Xbox Live. The consumer is part of a social setting of consumption that involves more than just advertising and products and services. As consumers we are affected by our close social groups and society, but we also dynamically affect them as well. It is pointless to discuss marketing in terms of brands creating meanings, associations and identities that consumers later adopt. The meaning of a brand is co-created with everyone in the consumer society who comes into contact with that particular brand.

Bought/paid, earned/non-paid and owned media communications

There is a fairly established way to categorize marketing communication channels within the marketing communication industry. It consists of the "trinity" of marketing communication channels: *bought/paid, earned/non-paid* and *owned* media.

Bought/paid media is essentially "advertising" – marketing communication exposed in media outlets in exchange for compensation or fees. It is called "paid media" since advertisers pay media channels for exposure. This is the most established, organized and dominant form of marketing communications, tracing back to the first half of the nineteenth century. Advertising, in all of its diversified forms still has by far the largest share of the global marketing communications market.

Earned/non-paid media is another type of marketing communications. This can be summarized as "publicity" or PR. The essence of the "non-paid media" label is the absence of direct payments for the use of media space. The typical standard non-paid media scenario is a "message" being voluntarily featured by various media channels – preferably journalists or media producers. The media channel spreads the message, but not to further commercial interests; it is instead driven by other reasons (e.g. public interest, journalism, popularity, information needs). This reverses the traditional advertising-based marketing communication process. Publicity/PR was historically used for political communications or by celebrities, and it is only recently, over the past twenty or thirty years, that it has been extensively adopted by consumer marketing communications. Commercial, consumer-oriented PR is now one of many established "tools" of modern marketing communications.

Since the term "non-paid media" assumes "paid media" (advertising) as the norm and mistakenly indicates the absence of payments (PR agencies do not work free), the PR industry questions this notion and suggests that it be replaced by the concept of "earned media". This stresses that PR communication is created by "earning" the attention of media producers and/or consumers. As a result, "paid media" become "bought media".

The final category, *owned media*, refers simply to media or communication channels that are owned or controlled by the author/brand/company/

organization/entity and that can be used to communicate with a desired audience/consumer/group/target audience. With the rise of digital media, as well as numerous social media platforms, the number of brand- and company-owned communication channels has multiplied dramatically. It should be noted that owned media can exist and have long existed in non-digital "offline" media formats – retail spaces, newsletters, loyalty programmes and many other forms.

Bought/paid, earned/non-paid and owned media are categories that can be used to understand how marketing communications work, but they also are fairly useful tools to consider when making creating a marketing communications strategy for a video game. Do you have the budget to create advertising and pay for the game's exposure in various media channels? Through which media channels do you expose your marketing message – television, magazines, newspapers, Web link advertising, social media advertising? Do you consider attracting attention to your game by means of PR and media relations? And finally, do you own or control any type of off- or online spaces that can be transformed into a media channel for your message – a popular social media account, a famous person ("brand ambassador") who can create attention, a conference, a LAN party, a Web forum, other games or apps, a game or other kind of store?

Four strategic communication models

Another noted way of understanding marketing communication is through the four models of public relations. This is a model that not only explains PR but can be used to explain how organizations, companies and brands relate to various publics or audiences. In line with this book, it has a company- or brand-centric perspective that focuses on how the *organization* relates to its public and audiences. The model has four categories: two one-way communication models (press agentry model, public information model) and two two-way communication models (asymmetrical model, symmetrical model).

The press agentry/publicity one-way communication model uses marketing communications to persuade and manipulate target group to interpret and behave the way the company or organization intends. The metaphor for this model can be propaganda and publicity stunts – any means necessary to put your message through. While many would instinctively consider this an outdated mode of communication in Western societies, it is alive and thriving in the marketing communications industry. A simple case: when Red Bull in 2012 on live Web video dropped a man from a balloon at 39 km altitude and broke the world record for highest altitude jump (and two other world records) in order to attract attention to Red Bull's "commitment to extreme sports", this was no different, in terms of communication logic, from most Cold War–era propaganda campaigns. The logic of publicity-based marketing communications is continuously reinvented in the marketing communication industry with new terms such as "event marketing", "action marketing", buzz marketing" and other types of communication concepts that focus on generating attention by means of events and actions that somehow are meant to stimulate sales.

The public information model evolved from the publicity model as it became understood that a more sophisticated approach was needed. In this model organizations started spreading accurate and (fairly) truthful information to various publics but mostly used media outlets to *inform* the public about the messages and intentions of the organization. The term "in-house journalism" is often used to explain this communication model. Its limitation was obviously the one-way communication aspect – the public is not always interested in being merely informed. Despite this, the model is still heavily used in contemporary media society by state agencies and large corporations for press releases. Bureaucratic organizations all rely heavily on this type of communication on a daily basis.

Communication evolved into the first two-way communication model – the asymmetrical model. This model is similar to the publicity model with the notable difference that *some* communication streams from the audience or public – but it is asymmetrical since the dominant communicator is still the organization. The views, opinions or messages of audiences were communicated only with the intention of "reducing the noise", as described previously. Communication from the audience is allowed only to improve the communication from the brand or organization. The company's goal is very often simply to reach as many people as possible in order to promote and to increase sales. This is the most dominant and most rapidly expanding mode of communication – in many way it *is* traditional and current marketing communications. The organization is the author – the audience is the public, and its opinions are interesting only as far as they help improve the company's efficiency, defined as getting audiences to do what they are being instructed to do. From one point of view this is a very outdated and almost arrogant model of marketing communication, since consumers are essentially treated as objects of a commercial type of propaganda. From a different perspective, the model constitutes one of the most legitimate things an organization can do in contemporary society – instrumentally manage its communication to achieve the business objective of reaching as many people as possible and prompt them to buy the product or service.

Despite the legitimacy and tradition of this model, there are clear signs that it is overused and becoming obsolete, for reasons explained earlier concerning the transition from one-to-many to many-to-many communication – society, technology, marketing and consumer culture have all shifted toward an individualistic and personalized era. This transformation is sometimes referred to as the two-way symmetrical model. In this communication model the asymmetry of the previous model has evolved into a model where the organization/brand/company and consumers/publics are on equal footing – all parties involved are considered authors as much as they are considered audiences/readers. Communication is used to negotiate with publics, resolve conflict and promote mutual understanding and respect between the organization and its public, according to a prominent definition. Although slightly utopian in its expectations that companies will be totally open and transparent with the public, which in today's business climate might seem naïve, the focus on balanced relationships via communication is indeed partially reflected in an age of social media, celebrity CEOs, dialogue-based marketing communications strategies and a general blurring of the boundaries between personal and private in terms of communication; most brands nowadays attempt to create an image of almost being their customers' personal social media "friend" rather than using an official one-way communication tone of voice. The preferred metaphor for two-way symmetrical communication model is simply "dialogue-based communication". Partially a vision of the future, rather than a description of modern marketing communications, the model points toward a future where communication will be based on relationships with different audiences, rather than one in which audience as seen as objects of a friendly and commercialized form of propaganda.

How do the four models of communication help us in the marketing of video games? In the next chapter we use these models, as well as the bought/paid, earned/non-paid and owned media perspectives, to look more closely at various type of marketing communications tools that can be used in video game marketing.

Advertising

It is important to clarify that most forms of marketing communications are frequently misunderstood as "ads" or "commercials". Advertising is limited to bought/paid media and involves one-way/asymmetrical two-way marketing communication. All other forms of marketing communications are often, from a pedestrian point of view, called "advertising" but cannot be considered as such strictly speaking. Therefore, we need to separate advertising from all other types of communication that aim to aid the marketing of goods and services.

There are countless types and categories of advertising. A traditional way to categorize advertising is according to media type – television, Internet, mobile, newspaper, magazine, outdoor/billboard, radio and cinema. But there are endless other ways to advertise, since the quest to find new advertising spaces is continuous and dynamic – some of these new spaces include graffiti, elevators, shopping cart handles, dozens of varieties of in-store advertising, public transportation, human billboards (probably the oldest form), bicycles, airplanes, balloons, and even face tattoos. There is no point in describing each and every one of these advertising forms, but there is a need to explain how they are managed in marketing communications.

Contemporary advertising can be described as bought/paid media and two-way asymmetrical communication, although to a lesser degree the two one-way communication models are also practiced. The most important thing to remember about advertising is that optimal exposure is the primary objective of advertising strategies. Therefore, all efforts are invested in reaching out with a clear and focused message – consumer dialogue and relationships are costly in terms of resources and time and must be limited. Advertising is about communicating in the mass media for a mass audiences, and using the most cost-efficient exposure medium is the primary objective.

In terms of advertising practice, a client can deal directly with an advertising media owner and buy space. But if a game developer or publisher wants a more professional approach to reach its target audience, it is wise to turn to an advertising agency. An advertising agency is primarily involved in the actual creation of an advertising idea or message and then producing it for the chosen advertising media channel. Historically, the advertising agency also helps in selecting and/or purchasing space in the media channel in which the client's advertisement should be exposed (print, television, radio, outdoor). As advertising media have grown and diversified, the function of advising clients on media selection has become increasingly complex, and some agencies have evolved into separate entities called media agencies. A media agency makes surveys, measures and analyzes various media audiences and their preferred media channels and consults on advertising media purchasing. Sometimes they are also active as resellers of media space, which they buy and sell, acting as intermediaries between media houses and (usually large) advertising buyers.

Advertising is obviously something that must be considered when developing a successful marketing strategy for a new game title. The high entry barriers in terms of advertising budgets make it prohibitively expensive for most small indie/ app game start-ups – but there are also highly targeted cost-efficient alternatives (such as the world's biggest text advertisement–based service, Google AdWords) or mobile advertising platforms. The previously explained components of a strategic marketing plan apply, including segmentation, target group identification, and in general the 4Ps of the marketing mix. All of these must be taken into consideration when using advertising as a marketing tool since, because of its mass communications approach, it requires quite substantial resources. Although advertising has since the nineteenth century been the cheapest way to increase sales of a product or service when costs are calculated per customer (so-called customer acquisition cost), total costs still add up when marketing to potential mass-market target groups of millions of consumers. But advertising can still be an extremely successful marketing strategy. Mobile game apps such as Mobile Strikes and Candy Crush Saga invest millions to promote their successful titles, but the indie hit Minecraft has barely used advertising at all. In other words, the strategic decision to use advertising depends on multiple factors such as marketing budget, sales objectives, potential market size, target group size, market geography, physical/digital distribution, local distributor partners and publisher strategies and resources.

PR/strategic communications

Public relations is sometimes referred to as *strategic communications*, and there is debate about what really constitutes PR, whether it is in fact different from strategic communications and how this all relates to marketing communications. Despite this confusion, generally PR and strategic communications are the management of communications from an organization to its audiences or public(s). This also involves internal communications within the organization (internal/organizational communication); communications with investors in a (publicly traded) corporation (IR – investor relations) or with public institutions, government agencies, political organizations (public affairs/government relations/lobbying); and communications during major organizational crises (crisis communications). These are valid dimensions of marketing communications but have less relevance for this book. Our focus is on the company or brand and how the organization communicates with its (consumer) audiences. Consumer/marketing PR is the field most relevant from a game developer perspective since it constitutes a tool in the arsenal of contemporary marketing communications. Strategic communications approach the challenges of PR in strategic, long-term fashion, as opposed to tactical, short-term and reaction-centred approaches to PR and communications that traditionally dominated the PR industry where organizations would bring in PR specialists to help with a crisis, press events, press releases and to manage media relations (e.g. arranging exclusive interviews). Nowadays PR is an established function within most consumer marketing–oriented companies and brands, and PR agencies and specialists partner with advertising agencies (and several other entities) in shaping the marketing communications strategies of companies and brands.

Within (consumer) PR, the approach covers the entire spectrum of communication models – from the one-way communication models of publicity through public information to the two-way asymmetrical and symmetrical models. PR covers earned/non-paid media and, to a large degree, owned media. In other words, PR covers a broader spectrum of media types and communication modes than advertising. Contemporary PR communications come closer than advertising to meeting and in certain cases fulfilling the vision of the symmetrical two-way communication mode, since its objective is to create long-term relations with consumers and audiences through any type of relevant communication activity that brings brands and companies and consumers into a dialogue. This activity ranges from the invention of attention–attracting stunts (such as Red Bull's record-breaking skydive), red-carpet VIP celebrity launch parties and celebrity-driven media-directed stunts to more long-term communication efforts such as driving a societal issue (such as The Body Shop's or Patagonia's environmental stance or Absolute Vodka's and Subaru's LGBT stance), creating forums for consumer dialogue, participating actively in (consumer) community dialogue when a major development is happening (e.g. construction of a new factory, real estate projects) or opening up for consumer dialogue as part of product development, arranging relevant public debates and so on.

Traditional PR focuses on the two one-way communicational models of publicity and public information, which are very much focused on generating public attention through the attention of mass-media professionals. The formal name for this is "media relations", which involves creating long-term relationships with journalists, reporters, celebrities, "opinion leaders" and any other professional who has access to the coveted exposure of mass-media channels. Frequently portrayed as manipulative and ethically dubious, the field of media relations is more accurately based on an "attention/information economy" of various influential professionals who work in PR inside media production and create its content (celebrities, politicians, opinion leaders), meaning that much of the discussion in media today is not unbiased and objective but orchestrated to achieve strategic objectives. Producing successful and popular media requires firsthand access to information, and if information sources are managed by a PR agency, then access must be negotiated to find a compromise between the (biased) view of the information source and the reporter/journalist, who may have his or her own agenda and may act as a kind of "filtration mechanism". Although this relationship is often portrayed as hostile, the truth is that the contemporary media/PR industry is characterized by a symbiosis between the PR world of content resource management and the world of successful/popular media production.

If done correctly, PR can be extremely cost-efficient in creating attention and establishing relationships with consumers in a much more dynamic and personal way than advertising does with mass-communications mechanisms. With the rise of the Internet, mobile devices and social media and a move toward a two-way communication-based media landscape (as discussed previously), PR is in a better position to adapt to this reality than is advertising, which relies on volume-oriented mass-media communication tools. Despite this, advertising still plays the biggest role in marketing communications – but PR has become an obligatory component, since big-budget marketing communications campaigns are rarely exclusively advertising based nowadays but also include a PR/strategic communications component. For instance, the action-film star Jean-Claude Van Damme was featured in 2013 in an advertisement for Volvo trucks in which he performed a split between two moving Volvo trucks. The advertisement was shown in a very limited way in paid media channels, but most of the marketing communications were done by PR specialists who created the right conditions for a media sensation, which was covered by countless established media channels all around the globe (the phenomenon of "going viral" is specific to digital marketing communications, which are discussed later). Without the advertising campaign, the PR campaign would not have succeeded – but without the considerably bigger PR campaign, this advertisement would probably have been forgotten as a fairly odd and expensive way of advertising the "dynamic steering" feature of Volvo trucks. In contemporary marketing communications the boundaries between advertising and PR/strategic communication are often very much blurred.

For a game developer, PR/strategic communications open up a range of possible ways to reach consumers. Most game developers can use PR/strategic communications as a means to reach a target group with marketing communications and also to reach target groups more cost-efficiently. Game culture has extremely dedicated consumers and gamers, and for many of them games are a way of life, rather than a product. Game developers are very much part of this subculture and know perfectly its specific cultural codes, characteristics, sensibilities and preferences. Reaching audiences by "seeding" screenshots and video footage of the game before its launch has become a video industry standard in terms of PR strategy – but there are more innovative ways of reaching the right game audiences. Every major game and genre has its own gamer audience, and the specifics of these are what successful PR strategies can identify and communicate in a much more fine-tuned way than having to speak to as many consumers as possible. A successful PR campaign speaks with *the right* consumers, not merely *as many* consumers as possible.

Digital marketing communications

As the entire media landscape has become digital, so too have marketing communications. This transformation has been the subject of much hype, many unrealistic expectations and a revolutionary thrill claiming that the digitalization of marketing communications has changed every assumption. This turned out to be, as always, a compromise between facts and misinterpretations. The truth is that no marketing communications in the Western world can exist without digital media communications. Creating successful marketing communications today means incorporating digital media the same way that an advertisement can switch from newspaper to magazine, simply changing media channel. But the Internet is not just one medium channel – it is constituted of hundreds upon hundreds of channels that sometimes overlap, sometimes are unique, sometimes are open, sometime closed, sometimes cooperate with each other, sometimes not, sometimes radically change and sometimes disappear – in other words, it is an ever-changing and mutating platform for an endless number of new media channels. This chapter separates "digital marketing communications" as this field is so vast, fast paced and technologically complex that extreme specialization is still required. This is also why digital marketing communications are part of every category of bought/paid, earned/non-paid and owned media communications.

The misinterpretation is based on revolutionary promises that still haven't been achieved after more than two decades of Internet-based marketing communications. Most of the marketing communications on the Web and mobile and social media are to a large extent created according to the same logic as nineteenth-century billboard advertising – to expose a message on a bought space to as many potential consumers as possible. Despite the huge innovation potential in marketing communications offered by Internet technology, most of the billions of euros in Internet advertising revenues generated by the likes of Google, Facebook and others are based on "virtual billboards" – banners, Web links and the selling of virtual spaces. What has radically changed, however, is the possibility of tracking, adapting and multiplying digital advertising spaces, as witnessed by the universal use of so-called cookies (Internet tracking software) by most websites in the world. But this adaptation, or rather the automatic mass production of countless niche advertising channels for exposure to potentially suitable audiences, is *not* about innovation of the advertising communication logic but about supercharging and pushing the advertising logic to its most extreme, mass-produced edge. Innovation in the future will come from focusing on the consumer and modifying the communication logic by means of content and its communication flows, rather than from the current advertiser focus on mass customization of traditional (albeit digital) advertising spaces and other advertising production factors.

The relational focus of PR is quite suitable to Internet-based marketing communications since digital media simplify finding, maintaining and developing dialogues through communities of like-minded people. Online communities have gone through multiple evolution stages but have during the past decade settled around the concept of "social networks". This turned out to be very compatible with PR communication logic since its approach builds on communicating through various off- or online social networks linking companies or brands and consumers but also consumers themselves. In other words, the arrival of various social networks has advanced new uses of PR in the digital realm, whereas advertising has advanced into social networks but primarily uses the same communication logic described previously.

The interaction-based nature of social networks has given rise to Internet-based "attention storms" where any catchy image, text or concept starts attracting attention in an accelerating spiral that creates instant fame and mini-fads. Tracking and database technologies allow us to explore these attention storms almost in real time, and this information can be used to super-charge the spiral even more once it has been recognized as such. These so-called virals become Internet phenomena that can rise and fall within hours, but, done properly, they can become global sensations that can drive attention and recognition toward a brand or company in a way that no offline advertising or PR campaign ever could. Creating the ultimate viral campaign has in many ways become the logic of successful digital marketing communications – to somehow combine catchy content with efficient technological sharing mechanisms but also with exposure to the right community that will start sharing. Sometimes this is referred to as *buzz marketing*. This is also the logic behind so-called *word-of-mouth marketing*, which studies how recommendations can become the best medium for successful PR-like marketing communications.

Marketing communications and beyond

As shown throughout this chapter, the lines that separate advertising, PR/strategic communications, and digital marketing communications are becoming increasingly open to question. Aren't there any new perspectives that attempt to somehow merge all of these? The answer is: yes, but not everyone agrees. The trend and consulting-driven marketing communication industry launches a new unifying concept almost every year, in an attempt to provide a new (and more profitable) way of defining (and selling) marketing communications. From a research point of view, a unifying perspective needs theoretical approaches *as well as* practical evidence. Therefore, there are only a few established unifying approaches, such as brand management, relationship marketing and integrated marketing communications. Branding, as already discussed, attempts to establish *brands* as the central concept of all of marketing communications. Many people would agree – but some people object to the practice of treating employees as "brand equity", and many organizations (e.g. public agencies or charities) do not identify with the set of theories and strategies that branding involves.

Relationship marketing is a perspective that emphasizes the importance of *relationships* as the foundation of all marketing communications. In some ways, it is very much the infusion of PR/strategic communication models into a marketing context. It was introduced in the 1990s and is built on the assumption that relationships must span the time *before*, *during*, and *after* the actual buyer decision process. Consumers and companies are organized according to long-term relationships, *not* according to short-term transactions and exchanges. Focus is put on dialogue, mutual interactions and problem solving, long-term perspectives, two-way communication approaches and, in general, communication *processes* instead of transactions. Relationship marketing is also more suited to service marketing, which, it argues, traditional marketing perspectives are not capable of explaining since they are based on product-oriented marketing approaches. This falls very much in line with the transformations of the contemporary media and consumer landscape that have been discussed in this chapter. Critics, however, raise the paradox that accompanies efforts to manage a relationship for profit – how can a company instruct and manage a profit-generating relationship that is supposed to be based on mutual interactions between company and consumers? In other words – how can you manage something that is not supposed to be managed?

Integrated Marketing Communications (IMC) is another approach to merging all of the various types of marketing communications. Whereas relationship marketing launched a new concept, this approach launches a strategy: to integrate and manage all and any types of communication activities that can affect the relationship between company or brand and consumers. Therefore it is more of a company managerial perspective, one that attempts to incorporate all types of established business functions such as distribution, advertising, PR, customer service, the sales force and market research in order to create one coherent management vision of how to always communicate with the consumer. Critics of this perspective point out that this perspective is indeed needed but that its ambition to manage the entire company and all or most of its divisions is slightly naïve since nearly every division in a corporation has its own answer for how to improve the management of the entire enterprise. Why would division managers suddenly accept a philosophy that calls for integrating everything under the management of the (integrated) marketing communications department?

The insight we can get from relationship marketing and IMC is the need within marketing communications to look beyond the boundaries of advertising and PR by unifying communication efforts and focusing on creating more long-term relationships between companies and consumers that are based on dialogue and more personalized communication channels.

Exercises

1   Analyze thoroughly a successful game and its marketing communications campaign. What type of media communications did the developer use? What about the four communication modes, advertising, PR/strategic communications and digital communications?
2   What kind of marketing communications would you use for your own game project?
3   Analyze the preferred media communications for various gamer target groups such as hardcore gamers, casual gamers or PC vs. console gamers

6 Marketing research for game development

Generating the data needed for decision making when marketing video games is pivotal for the success of game companies and the games they develop. The practice of generating knowledge for developing games is not something new to the industry but is something that today to a large degree informs the development of games. This same practice needs to be widened to understand your company's customer. This chapter presents an overview of the relationship between the marketing of video games and the information needed to understand consumers and the different markets. The chapter also discusses how this can be done within the confines of the company.

Learning objectives

1   To gain knowledge about and insight into the marketing research process
2   To understand what a marketing information system is and how it can be created
3   To learn how to conduct a research project for collecting, analyzing and presenting marketing research and insights

Introduction

How do you start making a game? Do you start at one end and hope that things will just fall into place when you reach the other side? Or do you sit down and plot the game, search for the information you need on different aspects of the game and, once you have all that information, start building the game? We would think that your game development falls toward this second description – that you find the information you need and use that information in order to create a game that meets the requirements you have set up. This could be research into technological possibilities for graphic, or AI. But it could also be research about the content of your games, about the real history that you are depicting in your game. This process of finding information and using it for game development is the topic for this chapter – but not information about the game itself, information about your consumers and markets.

Just as building a game needs to be based on accurate information, so do your marketing decisions. Finding the data you need is thus pivotal. But, these data need to be turned into information and then knowledge in order to be input to decision making. Much of what we have written in previous chapters deals with the point that any game developer needs to have a relationship with the consumers who it is hoped will buy the game. These are also the consumers that marketing communications are intended to address. In all of these occasions there is a need to have the right information about who your consumers are and about the market for which you are developing games.

Unfortunately, in marketing there are no single right answers like those that you might be used to from coding or from other technical aspects of game development. There are data that might or might not be accurate, but the knowledge that emerges from those data cannot be evaluated as right or wrong. The social sciences are by nature a relative science and by most measures also a constructivist science (more about that in Chapter 7). When it comes to scientific conclusions ("knowledge") about social phenomena, you have surely been told many times that "it all depends", that it's all relative. As much as that is true, it does not lead to a definitive base for decision making. You will probably agree with us that there is nothing more comforting than listening to a person who has all the answers, but in marketing there is no such thing as the right answer, and the persons telling you that there are are confusing educated guesses with facts. There are answers that are plausible and likely but never bulletproof, safe, 100 percent correct answers.

Marketing is, as a consequence, about doing the best with the data and information you have at hand. It is about using the data you can acquire or create on your own and turn into information that tells you something about those data. This information can provide you with further knowledge to make estimated guesses about the right marketing decisions for your company (see figure 6.1). This is called bounded rationality, and in the world of marketing you will need to get used to it. Because the rationales we employ are based on what we know at present.

As with any research in the social sciences, you need to remember the value of generating credible and reliable data. This will be the basis for your analysis,

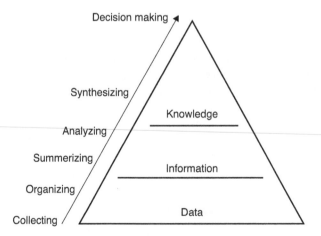

Figure 6.1 Data – information – knowledge

and the better the data, the more trustworthy and convincing your conclusions will be. There is consequently a huge benefit to be derived from investing both time and money in creating good data in marketing research.

What is marketing research?

Marketing research is a process that aims to support decision making in game development in order to facilitate increased market share, positive brand exposure, positive future sales or any other effect you want to achieve. It is not only about generating data about the consumer in order to know how to sell; it is also about generating data in order to build a long-term sustainable game development business.

The most successful game developers we have had contact with are spending much time and energy handling data about consumer, advertising, sales and other aspects of marketing. We expect that this is also the case with other successful developers. There are huge opportunities today to generate data about almost anything related to games. There are also analytical tools that can handle big data and provide statistical information that in turn can yield knowledge for decision making. No matter the size of your company, we strongly suggest that you get used to working with data about your consumers and your markets.

If you think about it, it makes much sense! Almost everything we do as gamers we do on digital platforms where we constantly share data with other consumers and the platform owner. These platforms have been set up by game developers like you. This presents you with ample opportunities to build a large number of nodes into your game systems for generating consumer behaviour data that you can export and turn into information, nodes from which consumers make decisions that affect improvements and success of a game.

There are opportunities today to use outside resources to carry out your marketing research. There are quite a few consultant companies that have comprehensive knowledge about doing this kind of research in both generating and analyzing data and industry knowledge from the video game industry. If you have the opportunity to use these services, we very much recommend it because of the significant added value for your game development. But at the same time we also strongly suggest that you be part of that research. Being a start-up or small developer, you will probably face a shortage of funding, meaning that you do have to provide this research yourself. The value of being part of the research process is that you get to know your consumers. For us, this is the best way of learning what works and what does not work with games: listening to consumers and sharing their experience of playing games. If you get too far from your consumers, you might risk losing sight of the kind of customer for whom you are making the game.

Marketing information systems

Figure 6.2 presents a marketing information system. It maps out the relationships among a game developer, the information needed and the external environment.

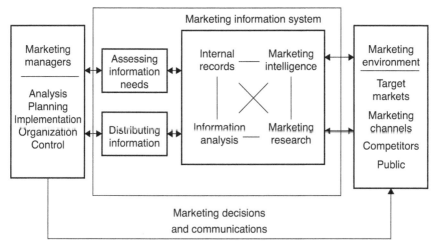

Figure 6.2 Marketing information system

Source: Kotler et al., 2008, p. 326

The marketing information system is, so to speak, what stands between you as a developer and the market. Getting the right information about the marketing environment increases the likelihood you will make successful decisions. There are a number of ways to handle these relationships. What we argue here is that, no matter the relationships, this needs to be formalized in order to ensure that information is part of decision making in the company.

At the core of any marketing information system is the generation of data for use in making marketing decisions. Through *internal databases, marketing intelligence* and *marketing research*, it is possible to assemble data and *information for analysis*. Each of these areas should be developed according to your company's needs. Generating data is generally no problem today; generating accurate and relevant data is a bigger problem. This is a result of the ease of accessing data, filtering out all the data that we do not need and isolating those we do need. Decisions should then be based on building information for decision making that makes sense for your company, where you are situated at the moment. A start-up does not need the same information as a more established developer, and a developer of casual games does not need the same information as a developer of games for consoles platforms.

Internal databases

Internal databases serve the purpose of gathering and storing data from processes within your company. Databases in a company have many sources and functions, from accounting to human resources and product development. As such, they are nothing new to game development. The function of these databases is to store data that can be used for strategic future decisions. These decisions may be financial, personnel related or product related. In any case the data serve the purpose of enabling informed decisions.

Having a clear strategy for what databases to create also requires decisions on how these databases relate to each other and how the data from the different databases are synthesized and compared. Companies like Ericsson, for example, use their databases on sales and financial results to make decisions on what personnel they will need in on a short-term basis. When connecting different databases, you thus enable a synthesis of data, both external and internal, that has the possibility of creating additional information in relation to the data. Remember that data become information only when they communicate something; otherwise, data are just data.

Marketing intelligence

The data you can create internally in the company need to be complemented by external data about the market and your competitors. Most of the persons we know who work in the game industry have a passion for games and are engaged in both reading and commenting on the industry. This is a good thing! It means that your information about what is happening in the game market should be up to date if you are investing the time to participate in the right communication channels.

Markets tend to be unique, meaning that there are different aspects that need to be part of your marketing intelligence depending on what market you target. But in general there is basic information that you need to have: you need to know how your *competitors* are performing and what other *games* are in the pipeline. You also need to gather information about what is happening in markets in terms of *technological development* and *legal aspects*. This information should constantly be updated to make sure that you are taking the right decisions.

The video game industry is extremely open and sharing with data and information, but at the same time it can also be closed and secretive. Being part of a hit-driven industry, most developers keep information about future games and new features to themselves. This is in the nature of a business where a feature can be copied fairly simply. But surely you have also have experienced the openness and sharing culture of game developers at industry conferences and online communities. The result is that much information about what is happening in different markets is available through industry conferences, industry newsfeeds, or other online sources. It thus makes good sense to attend conferences, not only for displaying your game but also for gathering information about what is happening and for building networks.

The two remaining components, *marketing research* and *information analysis*, are presented more extensively in the rest of this chapter, as they are part of the marketing research process.

Marketing research process

In addition to gathering information about your competitors and other aspects of your environment, you need to build knowledge about your consumers.

This is, we believe, where most of your effort should be invested. The types of research that you do are very much dependent on where in the production process you perform your search and what types of questions you want to get answers to. The different types of marketing research that you will need on a general level are pre-production, production and post-mortem marketing research. These are organized according to the internal (game) production process of your company/developer studio.

Pre-production marketing research is aimed at acquiring knowledge about potential consumers' needs and wants. You should plan and anticipate most of the relevant type of research that is possible to explore *before* you initiate the resource-intensive production/game development process. A dominant theme for this research type is related to issues of *rationalizing* the production decision, the estimated production resources and expected results (e.g. profit/loss, strategic implications). Standard areas of interest are target groups, market segmentation/area/size/demand/share, sales expectations/developments and consumer behaviour in general. Your information can be based on extensive primary data research (discussed later) or secondary data sources such as industry consultants, industry reports, open/closed databases, government agencies (particularly those interested in regional development, media/cultural industries and technological innovation), industry conferences, industry publications, academic journals, consumer trend reports, social media debates within relevant subgroupings, opinion leaders, and competitors and their marketing communications.

Production marketing research allows you to continuously generate knowledge about consumer behaviour in a game and also about what is happening in the marketplace, what your competitors are currently doing and how the marketing environment is evolving. In traditional AAA console game development, production marketing research is important, but once the production is initiated then the frames defined by the pre-production marketing research and production settings usually don't allow for major new strategic directions. In the contemporary game industry structure of game apps, social gaming, casual gaming, and freemium models with increased popularity of expansion packs and/or in-game purchases, the role of production marketing research has increased in importance. A service-dominant game industry and market (more about this in Chapter 3) has transformed production from intermittent development projects into a seemingly never-ending process of continuous development and upgrades, and this is also helping to transform the role of production marketing research.

Production marketing research is by definition based on internal production and is consequently more sensitive than aggregate industry data. It reveals a lot about the financial situation and performance of a game developer. As a result, these data are highly guarded and are acquired through proprietary primary data collection. In traditional game development, this involves data related to production resource utilization when reaching alpha, beta and gold version of the game software. In the current, more service-oriented game industry, there are more external sources of production marketing research data. With continuous upgrades and expansions to the game world, the market data become continuous. Business intelligence sources such as App Annie provide reliable marketing data that are relevant when making production decisions in the midst of the continuous-upgrade cycle of the contemporary game market.

Post-mortem marketing research generates knowledge about a game that has reached the end of its life cycle. The purpose is to learn from historical performance, successes and errors in order to generally improve the next game project and in particular to improve internal research data to use as input for the pre-production marketing research for the next development project. Post-mortem marketing research allows what the other research types don't – an opportunity to analyze a complete set of user and market data, making the information more comprehensive and allowing you to observe various trends, causal links and mistakes made during the entire life cycle of the game.

All of these types of research projects – pre-production, production and post-mortem marketing research – provide information that can improve your knowledge about consumers and therefore improve your game development process and increase the likelihood of success.

Problem definition

Most research projects follow a similar structure (see figure 6.3): problem definition, research plan, implementation and analysis. Coming from the world of university research, we value and appreciate well-defined problems. We know that this is not the case in industry where problems are something to be solved, not embraced – problems are seen as *problematic* instead as challenges that generate sources of insight and development. But you could and should appreciate that defining a relevant problem is just as important as finding a relevant answer. Having a clear understanding of what you want to find out also limits the risk of a situation where you make up the problem depending on what you find out – a trash-can kind of research-project metaphor. This is surprisingly quite common in the industry! These kinds of research projects are usually initiated on the basis of an apparent research problem. It seems almost as if defined by itself – "We need an answer to this problem because we want it solved and gone." This is a pragmatic problem looking for a quick answer to a "what, why, how, and when" kind of question. This question then demands that you pursue a research project in order to provide an

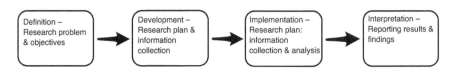

Figure 6.3 Marketing research process

answer. The charismatic Swedish sociologist Johan Asplund once suggested that doing research projects is very much like solving a murder mystery – was it the gardener or the cook who murdered Mrs. Smith? Continuing the analogy, the trash-can approach means that *there must be* a murderer – but what if it wasn't a murder but a suicide or merely an accident? A research question must be open to all eventualities and answers – including, and most importantly, the inconvenient ones.

Research plan

Depending on the question you formulate, you will end up needing different kinds of data. In general, research projects take a qualitative or quantitative approach, and these two create different data. A *qualitative* project aims at generating knowledge through understanding what people say or do and their relation to the research question, while *quantitative* research aims at quantifying data related to the research question in order to calculate knowledge regarding the question. Each of these approaches is valid – which one you use depends on the type of knowledge you intend to create. If you need to know how many consumers prefer certain aspects of games, you need to quantify the data. If you need to know consumers' preferences or thoughts about games, you probably need to talk to consumers in order to gain knowledge of why and how, instead of merely what. It is thus the research problem that defines the appropriate approach.

Creating a research plan involves planning for the data collection of *primary* and *secondary data*. No matter if you have a qualitative or quantitative approach, you are dependent on generating data that will enable you to analyze and draw conclusions. If you collect the data yourself, they are called *primary data*. If you use the data that someone else has created, these are *secondary data*. Both are equally valid, but if you are using secondary data you need to make sure that the data are reliable and provide you with the information you need. The data were probably created for another kind of research, so you need to apply secondary data in your research with that in mind. There are national and international databases available online that can provide useful information for your research projects. One example is the application App Annie (www.appannie.com), which provides information about games in Apple's App Store. But there are many other sources available to generate secondary data that will be useful in your research. Our suggestion is that you find sources that are reliable and useful specifically for your company and your market.

It is, however, important to distinguish between these two types of data, since they can seemingly overlap on occasion. For instance, a presentation by a self-proclaimed "game industry expert" at a game industry conference *might* be perceived as including primary data, since we are sitting in the audience in the front row listening intently. Despite this impression, they are secondary data – the expert is expressing his or her opinions and perspectives, and, no matter the speaker's fame and achievements, these conclusions can't be transformed into primary data. Frequently, this is the way opinions erroneously "turn into facts" and interesting research questions get bogged down in unsolvable debates, where primary data are scarce or unavailable and ignored. Primary data are those for which you as a marketing researcher have access to the research question with your own mind and eyes or for which you can verify every step of the way how the data were collected, analyzed and presented.

Implementation is the actual process of turning the research plan into action and reality. This involves collecting primary data sources, as well as secondary data sources, analyzing them and arriving at conclusions. This is frequently done with research companies that specialize in data collection tools, collection, and frequently also analysis. You need to be diligent in this process, since in the end consulting can indeed be outsourced but not the actual marketing decision making, which is squarely your responsibility, and blaming marketing research consultancies for your bad decisions is rarely a good excuse.

Analysis is the final stage of the marketing research process. It involves presenting conclusions and in most cases requires important decision making when it comes to the overall marketing process and the allocation of various resources. There are as many ways of analyzing data as there are research questions; in other words, analysis is highly adapted to the research question. It all depends on the type of game development, the expected target group, its segmentation, the potential market size, the overall game development budget, the geography of the intended market, the position of the game title in the game life cycle, the technology/game platform involved, the associated business model, competitors and their actions and numerous other strategic factors that all tie into a landscape that affects the type of research question and analysis that can be performed. Despite this, certain recurring themes can be identified in marketing research analysis: target group characteristics, target group awareness, estimated market area, total market demand, total sales, market share, future demand and target group future intentions. These and a number of other factors belong to the basic research data set of marketing researchers.

Marketing research methodology

Depending on the research question, you will use different research methodologies, as mentioned previously. Quantitative research methodology focuses on measuring and producing data in statistical terms in relation to research question, whereas qualitative research methodology provides descriptions as data that examine the *why* and *how* of a research problem. Methodology is dualistic in nature – it is very abstract and philosophical when it discusses fundamental assumptions about research as such, but at the same time it provides a very hands-on tool for collecting research data.

Focus groups are a qualitative research tool in which a fairly small group of people (depending on the research project and the number of subgroups, the sample can range up to several thousand prospective consumers) are asked questions regarding their opinions, perception and attitudes about a given product/service/brand/offering. The logic here is that the focus group represents certain dimensions of the general consumer population. By using focus groups, qualitative researchers can extract *how* consumers approach a specific brand and *why* they do so in a certain way. Depending on the research question, focus groups are meant to be more or less representative of a given dimension of the market/consumers (e.g. below a certain age). But qualitative focus group research is not meant to represent a perfectly and statistically proportional "mini version" of the market/target group through opinions that are statistically correlated with those of the entire population. For instance, instead of answering whether a majority of consumers are aware of the brand, qualitative focus group research can tell us about people's opinions and what they are based on, as voiced by those consumers negatively inclined toward the brand. This answers *why* and *how* some consumers have negative attitude toward a brand – but it does not with statistically certainty claim to reflect the opinions of the entire marketplace. Focus groups can also be analyzed with quantitative research tools in order to provide statistical perspectives on the opinions and preferences of the focus group. The important question here, as always with statistics, is the issue of representation – can the selected focus group be assumed to statistically correctly represent the entire population of the market/target group/market segment?

Interviews are, like focus groups, a predominantly qualitative research method. The purpose is also similar to that of focus groups, but with an individual focus that allows the researcher to dig even deeper into the rationale behind consumer attitudes. Interviews are one of the most versatile and most rewarding research methods, since they allow the researcher to interact with someone who, to some degree, has knowledge about the research question (or dimensions and parts thereof). This is truly the leading way to acquire profound knowledge about consumers. There are also quantitative interviews in which the interviewer follows an interview protocol; interviewee answers are immediately quantified into statistical data. Quantified interviews require large number of interviewee/respondent answers if the data are to be statistically significant.

Observations are, together with interviews, one of the most frequently employed qualitative methods within marketing research. An observer describes his or her observations in a structured way during exposure to a certain dimension of the research phenomenon. Observations have also become areas for quantitative research with the help of significantly more sophisticated technologies such as eye tracking or the use of numerous observation devices that are applied to the body of individual consumers as "wearables" in order to provide quantified data about the second-by-second well-being and performance of the body. Eye tracking is of particular relevance for game development marketing research, since this technology has already conquered the field of user interface design.

Questionnaires are mainly quantitative in terms of methodology, since the method requires respondents to answer questions without the presence of an interviewer; the data are more compatible with volume-focused quantitative research because of the streamlined and time-efficient way of collecting them. Questionnaires can also be analyzed qualitatively if the design of the questionnaire allows respondents to provide free-form text answers. With the rise of the Internet and the Web, the use of questionnaires has increased, since these digital media allow for the distribution of thousands of questionnaires within a matter of minutes. Collection and statistical analysis have become nearly fully automated as a result of this development.

Exercises

1   Create a research plan for your game project. Depending where you are in the production phase, you can choose to create research plans for the pre-production, production, or post-mortem marketing research types.
2   Make a general draft of the marketing information system that would be needed to provide data for your game project.
3   What kind of research data would you prefer – quantitative or qualitative? Please discuss your preferences, and make an attempt to explore the research option you didn't choose.

Part II
Challenge

7 Postmodern marketing

As a result of the modernism knowledge creation that swept across industries in the twentieth century, a postmodern understanding arose from different philosophers in the middle of the century. The ambition of the postmodern understanding was to offer something new as an alternative to modernistic thinking. This chapter offers a first alternative to the toolbox of marketing tools offered in the previous chapters. It also offers a first go at challenging our assumptions about marketing and markets.

Learning objectives

1 To understand postmodernism and the postmodern consumer
2 To appreciate the development from modern marketing theories to post-modern marketing theories
3 To gain insight into how postmodern thinking can create value in developing video games

Much of the knowledge that was developed about business and society after the birth of modern society aimed at providing knowledge for solving business and societal problems. By "modern society" we mean the society that had its origin at the start of the industrial revolution at the end of the eighteenth century in Great Britain and across Europe, a movement of industrial, cultural and technological change that fundamentally changed how we live and make a living.

The industrial revolution created huge changes in our cities, where people flooded to search for work at factories and other places. They thus left the self-sustaining farming life in the country. This in turn created the need for structures to market the mass-produced goods, including clothing and household items, that supported this new ways of life. Many of the modern marketplaces we see today were a result of these movements. The economy changed to offer employment positions, and the circulation of money was vastly expanded to most part of society and to markets that saw the light for the first time. In many ways it is possible to conclude that at this time the consumer was born!

Understanding this new society that was created has been at the heart of the work of many sociologists and other scholars. These scholars considered power relations, hierarchies, division of labour and so on. Universities started to grow faster, as a modern society needs an educated population in order to manage and further develop what had been started (although one should not forget that there are universities that predate the industrial revolution).

Marketing was one of the subjects that were born out of this movement, as were other business subjects, such as management, accounting and retail. Marketing, in its first framing, was about how smaller companies could compete with major monopolies and oligopolies. In that sense marketing was a pragmatic subject to help a business to grow. Unlike subjects such as sociology and philosophy, marketing was never started as a critique of society but maybe instead was a critique of business structures that excluded fair competition.

Much of the marketing knowledge that we today teach at universities and colleges is as modern as the knowledge from the early twentieth century. There are also strong opinions within many business schools that this is the main contribution of these schools: to be an influential and credible source of knowledge on how to conduct business in the modern world. This is also the dominant reason why thousands upon thousands of students attend business schools each year, seeking the knowledge the schools can offer and arming themselves for forthcoming battles in markets.

Much of what we have communicated throughout this book about marketing in the video game industry has the possibility of building, delivering and communicating your games in a successful manner. The tools are thus in line with a modern take on markets and society. Although the video game industry is part of the cultural industries, those that have high messaging values, the industry has incorporated modern ideas of society. There are forces that use games in order to challenge these structures, but they are external forces that are challenging the industry, rather than part of the industry. We believe that it is very important that marketing be part of challenging a modern society, part of questioning our ways and how these can be improved to create a better society. And as you will see, using ideas that challenge modern society has possibilities to enrich our understanding of marketing and especially of marketing video games.

The postmodern turn

The postmodern turn was initiated as a result of our modern understanding of society. Using modernism as a base, postmodernism built its critique on the knowledge produced under the modern umbrella. Postmodern thinking had a huge impact on many areas in the late twentieth century: architecture, the arts, literature, philosophy, history and others. One overall ambition of postmodern thinking has been to challenge what we take for granted, what we assume and incorporate in society as tradition, fact or belief. As such, postmodernism argues for a critical relationship toward society and our knowledge of society. Although this critique is under fire for being unproductive, we believe that the productivity of postmodernism is in its relentless scrutiny of our assumptions in the quest for creating multiple understandings and explanations.

Postmodernism thinking encourages what has been called radical pluralism. This means that there is no single truth but many truths to a fact. The meaning of this is that, by opening the layers of assumption that most knowledge laid upon us, postmodernism can challenge both fact and the resulting truth. If we embrace a view that there are many possible explanations, many truths, to anything, we open up for discussions why we understand as we do – and how our understanding of truth feeds more truth. The point is that all of these perspectives do coexist, and they can be allowed to coexist. Let us share one example of what this might look like.

In 1991 the French philosopher and sociologist Jean Baudrillard wrote three influential essays on the Gulf War that had been raging between 1990 and 1991 in Iraq and Kuwait. Being a scholar who supported a postmodern way of thinking, he built much of his argument on these lines of thoughts. The basic idea of these essays was provocatively presented in the title "The Gulf War Did Not Take Place". To nations that were just coming out of a war with thousands of deaths and massive destruction, this claim raised some eyebrows when it was published. The point, as argued by Baudrillard, that this was not a war but an atrocity that had masqueraded as a war. Given the overwhelming power of the American military, the Iraq forces were diminished to ashes in days. In addition, this was also the first war that was aired on media in the West 24/7, with journalists filming every bit of the action. The result is that what was mediated to the world was a view heavily influenced by media propaganda. So if there was a war in Iraq – who gets to decide what this war was like? There is thus no single truth about this war but different representatives of events that took place in Iraq and Kuwait between 1990 and 1991.

A postmodern approach to knowledge thus refutes the idea of grand narratives. These are the kind of explanations embraced by modernism explanations. To be fair, these are the narratives we have fed you up to this point. Grand narratives present explanations of a large number of events, simplified into something where all complexities are left out. What is left are containers of explanations that have been emptied of their diversity and that offer frameworks of grand explanations. A postmodern approach to complexities instead focuses on local explanations, on understanding local stories and on the building of narratives. Modernistic simplifications are thus avoided and a palette of descriptions can be offered that communicates complexities.

An example of this is how we understand history. From a postmodern perspective, it can be argued that history is something that is created now, in the sense not that what we do now will be history in the future but that our understanding of what has happened is formed now. So history is created now; we decide now what has happened and how we let it affect us today. What kind of history we address is in principle the same grand narratives, while a postmodern take lifts out the complexities and the local truth.

Take the history of video games, for example. How many narratives have not been created on how this industry has evolved? All narratives separately offer both a historical description and an explanation for what happened and what effect it had. All narratives obscure complexities in order to offer simplifications. When challenging these narratives with alternative writings, descriptions and explanations from alternatives voices, we can offer a postmodern reading of the history of video games. What are the different sources for understanding this history today, and what other voices could be offered to allow us to understand it?

Once we use postmodern approaches to open up explanations and theories that are presented as grand narratives, we can both challenge these narratives and offer alternative explanations. Both of these processes can individually and together create new knowledge. They can also disrupt present knowledge, leaving us without a safety net. This is also one of the critiques of postmodernism: that it tears apart and shreds without building. And yes, tearing apart is sometimes easier than building – and in building we do have to make assumptions in order to proceed. But, as in the case of the history of video games, our understanding of this, our narrating of this history, favours some actions while it shuns others. Our possibilities of building are thus affected by how we historicize the past.

This leads us to a concept that is at the core of postmodernism – discourses. We all deal with discourses daily, layers of them – overlapping and contradicting discourses. These are basically how we speak and write about different aspect of society, and in doing so we also reinforce and reconstruct the very same discourses we represent. In his inauguration speech after being appointed a professor at the Collège de France, Michel Foucault began with the problem of saying anything outside discourses, freeing oneself from the tyranny of discourses. In that sense we are constantly representing discourses, never building anew.

Since it is impossible to break free from discourses in speech and text, we can choose between two alternative readings. The first one is that of convenience, of the pragmatic use of building on what we know to strengthen these positions and incrementally build knowledge. In science this is what happens constantly, ideally. We take assumptions we hold as true and refine them and add to that knowledge. But, at the same time as this builds knowledge, it might also stall understanding and knowledge creation by isolating one truth as the real truth.

Let us go back to Foucault and his writing on one of these discourses in order to understand how this plays out in one specific setting. Throughout his career, Foucault devoted his writing and his public presence to exposing and challenging discourses that constructed different power relations. He did this in order to, as he said, uncover the truth. One of the cases Foucault described was that of the mentally ill. The understanding of mental illness has changed throughout history (by what account, you now ask). In rural areas, hundreds of years ago, before the industrial revolution and modern life, disturbed persons were understood as village fools. These were the persons who stood out in some way from the norm, although they were still cared for as part of the community. At one point it was decided that they were harmful to society, and they were put away in prisons. So they were removed from society, now cared for by institutions, locked up together with thieves and murderers. They did eventually get their own "prisons" – mental wards, still in the form of prisons, where the mentally ill were kept away from society. The way we relate to mental illness has changed; the discourse on mental illness has changed. Another very informative example is homosexuality, something about which there are a huge number of truths in different parts of society. Some people see homosexuality as a mental illness or even a physical illness, an abomination, a work of the devil, and other people see it as something you are born as, something as natural as heterosexuality. In Sweden homosexuality was defined an illness up until the late 1970s. One story is that one of the reasons for the elimination of this classification was the large number of persons who called in sick to work because they felt gay!

Even if wandering into mental illness and homosexuality takes us a tad far from game development, the argument is still valid – discourses have a huge effect on what we do and how we do it. The game industry has a large number of discourses on how things are, and these are reinforced by a large number of people acting in line with these discourses. One of them, one that the media keep coming back to, is the number of female gamers. You might discard this discussion as part of a gender discussion about the right of everyone, no matter whom, to participate in, make and play games. And, yes, it is part of that. But it is also part of how the video game industry constructs markets and keeps constructing the same markets. With a growing number of persons playing video games, statistics show that gender is no longer a valid factor in understanding the market for games. Women play almost as much as men! But do you address this issue when developing games? That should be part of making games, just like any other factor that defines consumers.

Sheri Granier (HerInteractive) once told the story of a person at a game company who told her, "I have more left-handed players than I have female players, and I don't make games for left-handed people. Why should I make games for you?" At that point women played games despite of how the games were communicating their content. But the point is: how does the video game industry understand female gamers? Does the discourse of female gamers limit the industry? This and many other discourses need to be exposed in game development in order to create and strengthen markets. A postmodern approach, we believe, can be instrumental in challenging what is taken for granted. One place to start is to challenge the way we understand consumers.

Postmodern consumers

In our modern understanding, the consumer is a rational individual (or bounded rational, using available but limited information to make decisions) who acts out of a need, finding different ways to satisfy this need – "I am thirsty; therefore I find the optimal solution of a beverage that will quench my thirst." Obviously this would be tap water. There are also different kinds of needs that have to be fulfilled, from the basic need for food and drink to self-actualization (as presented in Chapter 1). This has been the way consumers have been understood in modern times, as rational creatures that evaluate their options and satisfy their needs by choosing the most logic alternatives.

Marketing communications are then a matter of communicating the need that products and services satisfy – for example "use this dandruff shampoo to get rid of your dandruff." Consumption is yet another process in the sleep – work – leisure cycle that modern society has come to mean. Actually, shopping supports work – we consume what has previously been produced. When talking with our parents and grandparents about their lives, we will for the most part find this view of consumption confirmed. But at the same time we guess that you, if you were born in the 1990s or later, will not share this view.

Once a society has developed a basic standard of living, its patterns of consumptions change. In many of the western European countries and in North America this happened somewhere in the early 1980s, and several Asian countries followed soon after. Our economies were growing after the recessions of the late 1970s. Gross domestic product was increasing, and the unemployment rate was dropping. At this point there was also a liberalization of markets sweeping across the world, and privatization, monetization and profits were becoming fashionable to a larger extent. (I do hope you at this point look up from this text with an expression of doubt and fear in your face. Yes, it is true, we are here employing grand narratives – simplifications of a complex history in order to rush forward and make a point. We do hope you forgive us for this faux pas in a chapter on postmodernism.) From the 1980s on many of us had more money for consumption, and the result was that consumption was less aimed at satisfying direct needs and more to expose us to the experience of shopping. With this twist, the postmodern consumer was born.

Of course we still buy the same products to satisfy our hunger or to quench our thirst. But the sign value of what we bought was starting to become all the more important, and use value and exchange value were becoming less so. It was no longer about buying a phone but about buying the right(!) phone – the one that has the sign value you strive to communicate. And no, dandruff shampoo was no longer about dandruff only. It was about being socially stigmatized – use dandruff shampoo or you will not have any friends or girlfriends. And water is not best drunk from the tap but should come from a bottle with the brand boldly printed on it.

I shop; therefore I am. This is the slogan of the postmodern consumer. The impact of brands, for example, is becoming amplified as consumers today use brands to define who they are in relation to friends and everyone else (significant others). What kind of brands you wear on your body is a play with associations, using brand values to define your consumer identity. The differences between consumers are also increasing, and we are seeing a multitude of expressions that were never present in the old regime. These are consumer tribes that jointly construct values and organize themselves around certain brands and objects in order to form communities that support and strengthen their identities.

These changes in consumption patterns – from satisfying needs to creating identities, from use value to sign value – have created possibilities for new markets to form and for established markets to grow. The essence of this is that postmodern consumers engage in markets, they invest in markets and they are related to markets so that there is almost a symbiosis. There is not one understanding of these new markets, but many. Maybe as many as there are consumers? This means that markets might become harder to understand, as the consumer seems to be so easily moved from one market to another. But at the same time these consumers are also your biggest asset. Earn the trust of a postmodern consumer and you will have a devotee for life.

This is also something that should concern the video game industry. Not only are consumers today willing to spend more money on leisure and culture than ever before; they are also showing great diversity in what they play, how they play and when they play. A game consumer is no longer one thing; that single truth about gamers has been turned into thousand truths. Just as games are no longer one thing, the truth about games has for a long time been on the list of priorities of game scholars. But from a postmodern viewpoint: why look for one truth when in reality there are many? Just as markets in general have been fragmented, so have markets for games. There is no longer one market; there are thousands of markets waiting to be constructed out of the complexities of consumers and consumptions. These are great possibilities!

What about the Tamagotchi (Bandai)? What was this if not a product for the postmodern consumer, constantly engaged in the domestication of technology and of the game that was a pet – or the other way around? We believe that games like this are proof of the complexities of the markets of the postmodern consumer, where games can grow where there were no games before. Bandai basically constructed this market. In doing so it opened up relationships among technology, culture and the consumer that are still present – on almost every phone (something that has been highlighted further with the recent release of *Pokémon Go*). We believe this is what we need to adapt and learn from postmodernism, that there are markets beyond our assumptions of what constitutes a market. And we must unlearn from modernism the idea that markets are found out "there" – which has us spending much of our time finding markets instead of making markets.

Postmodern game development

There are a number of ways to use postmodern thinking in the video game industry. Mainly we believe that it has the possibility to challenge thinking in the industry that limits its sense of possibilities. We are no longer looking for truth; we are looking for multiple truths. We know we are risking sounding unspecific and using a big brush to paint the picture and that at the same time the philosophically adept reader will sneer at our simplifications and translations of concepts here. No matter on which side of this you land, we would like to offer you some guidelines as you start to work through your game development.

All game development contains *explicit* and *implicit norms*. These are things that all of us assume. But explicit norms make our assumptions visible. We talk about them and make them a focus of our attention. They need to be there, and we need to talk about them. Implicit norms are also present to the same extent, but the danger of these is that we do not talk about them. We might not be aware of them, and they are many times hard to put into words. When constructing games, we need to be open about both explicit and implicit assumptions. So you need to create a structure in which you have the possibility to expose and discuss assumptions.

Categorization and *vocabulary* are the basis for knowledge construction. These two concepts order different arguments and objects so that they become as one another or the opposite of one another. There is a comfort in this, and it makes it easier for us to build new knowledge. We do not question the base on which we build this. But at the same time what we build will to a large extent be based on that foundation. So question the categories and vocabularies used. Words do have a meaning, and they build more truth.

The topic of *stereotyping*, *differences* and *otherness* is definitely not something new to the video game industry. These also communicate knowledge and values that belong to a modern world, not our postmodern one. A stereotype is a simplification beyond recognition, recognized by all but fostering identification with none. The grand narratives of stereotypes may no longer have a place in video games. It is not the known and the general that are of interest but the complexities and multiplicities of lived experience that create value. There needs to be a realization of what types of stereotypes you are building and why – what role they play and whether these really have the intended value you seek.

Exercises

1   What norms do you think persist in the video game industry: about the different consumers and about game development? What norms do you think exist in society about games and gaming?
2   What stereotypes are most present in the games you are developing, and why is this?
3   If you were challenged to develop a concept for a game that will break the present norms today, what would it look like? Why would this game challenge present norms?

8 Marketing as practice

Marketing is not only a pragmatic toolbox full of tools to handle markets and marketing. It also offers perspectives on understanding what an organization does and what consumers do. The aim of this chapter is to describe the knowledge gained from studies of marketing practices: where these ideas come from, how they are applied in marketing and what game developers can learn from this.

Learning objectives

1   To understand practice theories and how these have influenced marketing
2   To learn a few concepts that are critical in understanding and describing practice theories
3   To attain knowledge to let you start analyzing your game development as a practice

How is knowledge constructed? This rather obscure and philosophical question was explored in France by two researchers, Bruno Latour and Michel Callon. The focus for their studies was both how knowledge was constructed in science and how markets were constructed. What was different about these studies compared to previous studies was that they focused to a large extent on the very practicalities of creating knowledge and markets. The topic was no longer a philosophical discussion that had been taking place since the dawn of human thinking – what is reality, and what is knowledge? It became a here-and-now kind of approach to knowledge construction.

What was set in motion was a research field that is called Actor-Network Theory (ANT). This field has achieved a huge success in a number of difference sciences, including the social sciences (of which marketing is a part). The structures provided by ANT for understanding the effect of our interaction are profound and offer new and fruitful ways of framing many of our social interactions. At this point ANT has been incorporated into marketing as part of a practice movement, offering the value of understanding what is happening in markets in real, practical terms. This practice movement study, just as the name says, practices. That is: how are markets constructed in practice? One of the main suggestions made by this school is that we should become ants (ANTs) when trying to make sense of what is happening in marketplaces (or any other places). When we said that marketing offers pragmatic tools that help us understand and act when doing marketing, we also said that marketing is a way of thinking. Just as postmodern thinking suggests that there are more dimensions to marketing, we believe that practice studies have the potential of affecting marketing practices to a larger degree than it has so far. At this point there have been few attempts, to our knowledge, to translate this knowledge into useful practical suggestions for marketing students. That is what we are attempting in this chapter, and we are convinced that when you read this book five or ten years from now practice theories will be more present in marketing knowledge than they are today (although there is an obvious problem in providing practical tools that will be universal). Before presenting a practical application of practice studies, we take you down the road a bit on this kind of knowledge – so please bear with us.

One of the key arguments from practice studies is that the setting we call a market is composed of a large number of actors, both human and non-human. These actors are related to each other; they act toward each other, and they react on what other actors do. So when an actor does something, that actor engages other actors – he or she enrolls other actors to use ANT vocabulary, and the event is translated by other actors into a chain of events. It could be compared with a football match, where at the start a football player kicks the ball. This sets in motion reactions from other players on the field, who position themselves for that first action. They are, so to speak, affected by that very act of that first football player. What then happens with the ball and the game is a result of how all actors (football players) relate to other actors, including the ball, of course. The result of a football match is then not the act of that first player who kicked the ball but the acts of all actors involved in the network that is created as actors are involved in the unfolding of events.

In ANT any setting is composed of both human and non-human actors, including markets, game developers and any other settings you are involved in. Commonly in the social sciences the non-human artifacts have been strangely absent (if present, the non-human actor is sentenced to have a life as a slave to the human actors); in other areas it might be the opposite situation and humans are strangely absent. But when making sense of social (social is defined as including objects) interaction, practice studies mean to include both human and non-human actors – both persons and objects. The argument is that objects, things, have a very real effect on other actors (it would in other instances be defined as the environment of actors, but as this is composed of more actors, there is no such thing in ANT). Objects thus make us do things. This is an effect of how they were designed, how they were constructed, as whenever we build objects we inscribe them with programs of actions. That is, we code them to behave in certain ways. These programs then prescribe certain behaviour for other actors.

A classic example used by Bruno Latour is that of a sleeping policeman – this is presumably what a road bump is called if you translate the French name. If you have as a goal to get people to slow down when driving cars in an area, you have a number of choices how to enforce that. The best would, of course, be to have a policeman standing around; everyone would slow down! After this optimal alternative, one could imagine a sliding scale of solutions that would have an impact, slowing drivers to a diminishing degree: from the actual policeman to a cutout of a policeman, a flag-waving robot, and a sign. What policemen do very well if they are present is enforce a behaviour on the driver but also punish drivers who do not comply with the order to slow down – by handing out fines. The other replacements may or may not have the wanted effect, but they do not have the same force as the policeman.

Now, let us consider the road bump. The argument here is that most of the features a policeman has, the programs of the policeman, are actually built into the road bump. This means that replacing a policeman with a road bump would yield a similar result – people would slow down. The programs are inscribed into the road bump. So there is, in a very real sense, a program that will punish you if you drive too fast. There are no fines, but you end up with a damaged car. The takeaway is that artifacts can be inscribed with programs that have a real effect on other actors. The road bump will make you slow down, just as a policeman will make you slow down.

When talking about any actor, such as a sleeping policeman or a car for that matter, it is possible to zoom in and out in order to makes sense of the associations between actors and their relationships. For example, a car going over a sleeping policeman could be understood as an actor in a scene with both human and non-human actors, the driver and the car. Zooming in further enables us to distinguish different actors in the car, non-human actors: an engine, seats and wheels. We could zoom in even further: a piston moving inside a combustion chamber, connected to a crankshaft and so on. We could do the same with human actors: muscle, heart, lungs and so on. Thus, when we open up an actor, we find more actors! We could also zoom out: car industry, roads, car manufacturer, petrol industry and so on. An actor network could be used to close boxes of actors, thus constructing meta-actors and enabling the analysis of many different actors.

These aspects of practice theories, how practice affects actions and what kind of actors one should include, have had an impact on how we understand marketing and markets. There is a strong relationship with what we argued in the introduction of this book – that markets are not something that is out there somewhere but something that we construct and have an impact on when we support them through our actions. Just like any market, the video game industry is made up of a large number of actors, both human and non-human. Actually this industry is one that embraces non-human actors – an industry that actually is all about constructing actors, in games! So at the same time that the industry is constructed of these actors, the outcome is yet another actor that will prescribe actions on gamers and other actors wherever the game is present.

On fish, tomato and groceries

Let us provide you with three cases on how to understand market construction from the perspective of practice theories: the Indian fish market, the French tomato market and the transformation of grocery stores. We are in no way claiming that there are any similarities across markets (although some games do smell), but when it comes to understanding markets and market formations, there are clear similarities between tomatoes, fish and shelves and the video game market. Once we have presented these three ways to understand markets, we will apply this on the game industry.

To start with, fish. The Indian fish market is a large market. There are a number of different segments, from industrial fishermen to traditional fishing. But to a large extent these fishermen made use of traditional technology, both for fishing and for navigation. As modern technology, non-human actors, has been introduced, the market has changed, with economic and cultural effects. One technology has also changed the fundamental workings of that market – the possibilities to keep tap on prices online while still out at sea. It used to be the case that fishermen were limited to whatever price they were offered for their fish, depending on which harbour they decided to dock in. The price was also different at different harbours and cities, just as it fluctuated during the week. This market was offered the possibility to use mobile technology to scan prices offered at different harbours. The effect this had was that the fishermen could decide what harbour they would dock in, depending on the price, when they were still at sea. The introduction of this actor into this market thus changed the configuration of the market, what actors were present and the effect they had on the network of actors. The takeaway from this case is the fact that markets consist of a large number of actors, both human and non-human, and the configuration of a market is dependent on all actors. Introduce a new actor and the configuration of the market changes.

The second case is about tomatoes. The tomato market in southern France used to be structured by buyers travelling to different farmers, inspecting their crops and offering prices. These were local buyers, having contact with local farmers. The prices that were negotiated had little relation to those offered to other farmers with other crops. The power to define price and revenue for the farmer was in the hand of the buyer. In order to reconstruct this market and enable a situation where the price were more competitive and the farmers were not subjects to the whims and haggling power of a buyer, auctioning halls were constructed where all farmers could deliver samples of their crops for inspection. The marketplace also contained a bidding hall, and there was a process for buyers to bid on different crops. The result was a market with other settings, where the power was transferred to the bidders and tomatoes were compared and made available for everyone to evaluate. The actors involved thus changed, as did many of the actions that previously were part of the French tomato market. In understanding these changes from a practice perspective, we see the changes in the relationships between human and non-human actors that help us to understand how markets change or are changed.

The third case is not as specific as the first two. But it describes how actors change over time in a market, and the marketplace constantly changes just because of this. Grocery stores have always been part of how we buy food. They have formed our childhoods, and they continue to have a huge impact on our daily lives as adults. These places have developed quite substantially from the nineteenth century on. Grocery stores used to sell food over the counter; you had to talk to the shopkeeper and explain what you wanted. When mass consumption took off in the twentieth century, there was a need to change how consumers interacted with goods and how they bought. Thus the layout of stores was changed, from over-the-counter service to the self-service we know today. The effects were far reaching for a huge number of actors. The number of human actors, the consumers and persons involved in the grocery market, increased, as did the number of professions involved in selling grocery. The consumption patterns of consumers changed – how we shopped, when we shopped and why. Strolling along the aisles of food in stores is now possible and you can touch and feel the food. Thus the meaning of shopping changed, as it did for other products as well: clothes, technology and so on. Non-humans actors were enrolled to contribute in changing the network of actors: electronic price tags, self-checkout, the shopping trolley, plastic bags, frequent buyer card and so on. Thus the network of actors we are meeting when shopping for groceries is vastly different from what it was in the nineteenth century.

Understanding game development as consumer development

So what does this has to do with developing video games, you might ask yourself. Well, as it turns out, quite a lot. Applying a practice understanding to the video game industry has the possibility of highlighting actors, human and non-human, and relationships in the industry, the networks of actors that form the industry. This leads us to the understanding that changes in the configuration of these actors produce changes in the industry. It is possible to start making sense of how the industry constructs the market by understanding the actors involved and what they do, either zooming out and understanding macro actors such as industry structure, producers, developers and platforms or zooming in to understand how features in a specific game take part in structuring the industry through how it engages the consumer and micro transactions.

One aspect of the development of the video game industry is that there has been a long line of technological innovations that have been made part of the industry, just as there have been innovations that have been part of other industries, such as the defence industry. Using the concept of configurations of human and non-human actors, it is possible to do an alternative reading of this development as the development not of technology, but of consumers. Just as in the preceding chapter on postmodern theory consumers are in the centre of marketing understandings, in practice theories a consumer is but one of the actors on a market.

Now the introduction of video games is becoming a distant moment in our history. Although neither historians nor passionate patrons of video games agree on exactly when this development began, it is safe to say that the prerequisite for any of these games to exist was the introduction of computers with a graphical interface and enough processing speed to enable gaming. These innovations put us somewhere in the vicinity of 1950 to 1960, when bulky so-called minicomputers made their entrance onto university campuses and government facilities. No matter the exact point of introduction; it is astonishing that something that began more than fifty years ago has developed into an industry that surpasses the Hollywood film industry financially and has built a market that involves a majority of us – young and old.

The video game industry has a long history of technological development, encompassing seven periods in which technological innovation had a major impact on the relationship between game technology and the gamer. These periods are not necessarily sequential; they all have a loose point of origin and a progression that coincides with later periods. This lack of chronology exists because gaming technology converged through various innovations and their adaptations. The first period was initiated in the early 1960s by the development of *minicomputers*, acquired and used in universities and government agencies, where students and staff had the opportunity to create programmes, including games, for these computers. The second period started in the early 1970s, when coin-operated *arcade machines* were introduced as a means of playing games. This technology offered the consumption of games in a public setting, without the opportunity to create or modify the programme. The third period began in the early 1980s, when technology enabled gaming in a private setting as *home entertainment*. Through technological innovations, games could now be played on gaming consoles connected to the home television. The fourth period was introduced at the end of the 1980s through *handheld technology*, enabling consumers to bring games with them wherever they went: in private, public or professional settings. The fifth period coincides with or progressed in proximity to the fourth. In the early 1980s, the *personal computer* became available to households, enabling both a private interaction with games and the possibility of modifying their content. The sixth period, in the late 1990s, brought the introduction of *mobile phones*, and these devices offered a screen sophisticated enough for playing games. The seventh period, that of *smartphones*, was launched with the introduction of iOS and the App Store. To date, all these technologies, with the exception of minicomputers, are still available as gaming platforms.

What we have then are seven different configurations of human and non-human actors that at different points in the history of game development constructed the market. Some of these configurations still exist today in parallel, creating different parts of the game industry. But, consumers of video games were not the same in the early days of gaming as they are today. There are major difference among using coin-operated arcade machines at the mall with your friend, using the gaming console at home in the living room while competing for screen time and playing on your mobile while on your way to work. The different actors fundamentally construct different markets.

So, when understanding the development of video games, we need to change our focus from developing games to developing consumers. We do realize that none of you ever dream of constructing consumers when dreaming about your future, assuming that this is more in line with making games, or something similar. But if you think about it, if you aim to create a company that can sustain a continuous business of making games, does it not make more sense to create your consumers too? Again, look at the Tamagotchi. These consumers were nowhere to be seen before this non-human actor was put in the hands of the children (and adults) who consumed them. What Bandai succeeded with was creating a very successful assemblage of human and non-human actors where the connections between these actors were strong enough to reinforce the actors and translate the acts of the other actors.

Using practice theory for game development

Compared with the pragmatic toolbox we presented in the first part of this book, practice theories cannot be applied in a simplified model used to structure what we meet when developing games. What practice theories can do it provide us with is, just as in the case of postmodern theory, a critical approach in how the practice of video game development constructs markets and consumers.

The tools that practice theories offer us shift our attention from pragmatic tool to the assemblages that we construct when developing games. It changes the game from an isolated actor to a network of human and non-human actors that should form strong connections. Zooming in, an analysis would form the understanding of each actor in the game – graphic, feature and code support one another. Zooming out again, there are the game and the gamer relationship, relationships to micro transactions, online communities, consumer support and so on. Also understanding the company as such could be achieved by laying out the actors in your market: competitors, consumers, retailers, and so on. All of these actors are together creating the market you are looking at.

We do realize that working on game development is the opposite of being ants. But in order to understand the network you are part in creating when making games, there should also be the understanding that there should be times for ANTs. What an ANT sees is quite different from what the rest of us notice. The outcome of this work, we believe, can lead to a better understanding of the practice you are involved in at the moment, how it works and why it works. But at the same time this analysis has the possibility of opening up possibilities for new actors to be enrolled in your network. And constantly being adaptive and able to spot new possible connections and discard defunct connections is in the best interest of any business, not the least the business of constructing video game consumers.

Exercises

1 How is your company/team configured when developing games? What are the actors involved, and how are they related?
2 How would you map out the actors involved in your game development on a time scale? This map should show the possible chain of translations.
3 What actors outside your company/team do you involve when developing games, and what are their actions?

9 The future of game development

There are many challenges that lie ahead for the video game industry. We believe that there is huge potential for this industry to create a medium that is inclusive and interesting. But there are also threats that could lead to the building of a regressive industry. In this chapter we offer our view on the future. But, as a wise man once told us: it is hard to make predictions, especially about the future.

Learning objectives

1 To gain an understanding of where the video game industry has come from and how it is positioned today
2 To appreciate the challenges for the industry in the years to come
3 To rethink your role in this future

The video game industry has many times been compared with the film industry, for both the similarities of the products and the similarities of their industry structure. What we need to remember is that the video game industry is a younger industry than the film industry. Film was introduced in the nineteenth century and started to make its mark internationally early in the twentieth century. This means that the film industry is more than 100 years old, maybe as old as 120 years old. The start of any industry is diffuse at best. Looking at the video game industry as it grew out of tinkering with machines after World War II, we can trace it to the beginning of the 1970s. With an estimated history of forty to forty-five years, a comparison both builds unfair expectations and unfair expectations for what lies ahead for the video game industry.

One comparison with the film industry that for us describes the problems for the video game industry is that the video game industry is today where the film industry was in the beginning of its history – not yet structured and in the phase when roles and relations within the industry evolve. At the same time games have been viewed as similar to the film of that era – as showing a fascination with train wrecks, car crashes and poor narratives. Leaving aside whether this comparison is fair to the video games industry or to films from that time period, it emphasizes the problem of taking a medium and an industry and helping it grow into something that transcends the initial fascination and making it into a medium that has the capacity to explore different aspects of society and activities. For the video game industry this is reflected quite well in challenges to create inclusive cultures for developing games and to develop inclusive games that tell stories other than those of conflict and war.

The video game industry is about both games and the structure of an industry. There is no way to separate these two. There is thus much reason to include both of these aspects when trying to understand where the industry is positioned at the moment and also where it is going. When trying to make sense of other industries, we often focus on three aspects that influence their development: *economy*, *technology* and *culture*. These three aspects are general drivers of change, and to limit our consideration to only one of these three would also limit our understanding of the future of the industry.

Looking as the development of the industry thus far, we see that these three aspects can to a large extent help us to make sense of its position. The video game industry, like many others, is defined by economic possibilities. Knowing how much money is available for developers in term of state funding or private funding and investment is one way of looking at financial possibilities. The liberal movement in early 1980s had a huge effect on many cultural industries, as there were more privatizations going on. Theatre, opera houses and other institutions were moved into private spheres, with the expectation that they would make money filling seats. The effect of this on the video game industry has to be understood as the result of new cultural offerings competing for consumer spending. Video game development did not have state ownership at the start as did many other cultural industries. As a matter of fact, in the early years of game development, the industry was having problems defining what kind of industry it actually was – software, culture, toy or something else. Today there is greater acceptance of the video game industry, but in many aspects the categorization problem is still present. It has been defined as belonging to creative industries. We believe this concept is misleading (more about this categorization later) and would rather see a definition of the video game industry as part of cultural industries. But industry categorization has an effect on how we understand practices and outcomes in that industry. For the video game industry this had a real impact in the early twenty-first century, when much money was invested in the software industries. As part of the huge Internet hype where everything seemed to be possible, if one only spread some Internet on your business it will succeed. Video games are not part of the Internet; it uses the Internet for distribution and communication. No matter this difference, the video game industry attracted many participants who subsequently were affected when the bubble burst.

In a sense technology has always been the beginning and the end of video games. If we look at the hack at MIT, Spacewar!, that was all about technology. The video game industry is thus heavily dependent on technological possibilities and developments in game delivery. But technology can never be the only narrative when telling stories about the development of the video game industry. Although the industry is heavily dependent on technological skills in order to deliver games, games as such are not dependent on technology – well, digital technology at least. Games are dependent on a set of agreed rules and the tools needed to set up challenges. But it is impossible to understand this industry without understanding technological development and how each technology presents different possibilities for bringing games to consumers. Depending on what the technological possibilities were, the different games that we have seen have shifted from arcade, to console, to mobile and other applications. To a large extent technology has also been allowed to be the driver of game development, and new features in games can be attributed to new technological possibilities rather than to alternative ways to conceptualize play or narratives. But at this point in the industry's development technology has brought games to a point where everyone can play almost anywhere. It is an enormous feat, if you think about it!

The last puzzle in understanding the video game industry is how cultural changes have affected the development of the industry. The cultural difference in playing video games today and playing them in the early 1970s is remarkable. But this development is not isolated but is part of major changes on consumption and societal changes. In general there has been a change from consumption as part of a practical aspect of your daily life to consumption as an activity that you can indulge in because of the experience itself. This has resulted in making more money available for consumption of cultural good, including video games. So the category of products that includes games has been growing, thus driving cultural change and acceptance of the presence and consumption of games. This, together with the growth of generation G, described in the introduction, has changed our perception of game consumers – gamers. Of course there are geographical differences. Games do have different status on different regions. But we would claim that playing video games is not as stigmatized as kid's play as it was back in the 1970s. Although many of us playing Candy Crush or Word Feud on busses and subways would not define our self as gamers, we are still using games in our daily consumption. This cultural change has also had an effect on knowledge about games, making it possible in the early twenty-first century to build research programs about games all over the world. These are invaluable in providing knowledge about game and game culture, just as film studies provides knowledge about that medium.

In order to understand the future of video games, we need to understand the past. We know that there are many stories about the industry and how it came to be, and using economic, technological and cultural explanations is but one way of framing this history. For us, the takeaway is that there are a few areas in the future that we think will be critical for the development of the industry. This list is in no way exhaustive, but it provides a basis for us to think about the industry.

Inclusive game development

A theme that runs deep through the video game development is that of cultural appropriation of game developers. Our experience is that developers love talking about those crazy days when the studios were all fun and games: loud music, indoor skateboarding, sleeping on the office sofa, drinking an insane amount of Coke, and so on. There are even books on this topic! These are biographies that construct a cultural backdrop for developers to embrace, although we never saw any of these studios ourselves, only professional workspaces like those in many other industries with computers, sketches, social space and the sound of people working. Stories about the past have a very real effect on how we behave today. They build a culture of historical heritage that communicates about right and wrong. Remember all those stories your parents read you as a kid and that were educational in socializing you into society. These stories, we believe, are instrumental in building a strong community force for game development and in creating an *us*. They also ensure that we do not exclude potential new sources – fascinating people, ideas and games.

The problem is thus not that there is a strong cultural history in the industry but how this plays out today. A strong culture can unite and strengthen both the product brand and the employer brand of any developer. But in the case of video game developers, this culture is very homogeneous: male, white, young, and middle class. Of course, there are differences that we all can point out to among different developers. And that is a good thing! But the question is whether that changes the culture or whether persons who do not belong to the culture are forced to play along to be accepted.

The effect can be seen both on the games that the industry builds and on the persons who choose to engage in this industry. Some of the problems that the industry faces are part of a major challenge for technology and social structures. We know that there is knowledge in the industry about these problems, but we also think that we can do more.

The first challenge for inclusive game development is the games that we today see on the market. Given this homogeneous group of persons employed in the video game industry today, it is a bit of a stretch to argue that they have the knowledge to build games that are interesting for other segments of consumers. If we trust the statistics that come out of trade organizations and other research facilities, the audience that today plays games – the ones we call gamers – runs from toddlers to senior citizens. They are both men and women. They come from all corners of society. So how does the game industry reinvent itself and make products that are interesting for people besides the hard-core gamers, the already devoted?

Again, compare this to the film industry, where the number of genres and productions is much wider than for games, taking into account that games as a medium have much greater possibilities to communicate images, sounds, movements and interaction than films. What is stopping the industry from building games for everyone? The recent push of casual gaming we believe is showing the possibilities for other segments to engage with games. Continuing to build on that, we think, could prove a future challenge.

Knowing your consumers means reaching beyond knowing yourself as a developer and your preferences. In the 1980s the clothing industry felt that it was losing touch with its consumers. At that point the persons working in the industry did not represent the consumers who actually bought their products. This is somewhat the same situation as the one that prevails in the video game industry today. At that point, reconnecting to the clothing market became very important. One of the solutions was to use trend spotters, persons who are very much involved in the market that you are targeting. For these manufacturers they targeted the trendy, aware young people with disposable income to buy clothing and to party. By having these trend spotters engaging in these environments and reporting back, the manufacturers could know what was in fashion and what was coming into fashion. So how do game developers spot these trends? Or does the game industry construct these trends themselves? Keeping in touch with consumers in your market is pivotal.

If there is a challenge in taking games to a wider audience, does that mean that the persons developing games have to change? There is no easy answer to this question. But it follows the same logic as many other discussions about diversity and culture. If quotation into company boards creates better boards and so on. No one simple knows. The idea is that a more diverse set of individuals can offer different perspectives on any process or decision, which leads to better decisions. Remember that this question is not only about gender, although only 10–15 percent of employees in the industry are women. It is about including persons with a wide set of characteristics who together can construct diverse teams. The idea is that the organization's staff almost mirrors the consumer base. Now this is a hard feat to achieve, even if it is desirable. What needs to be achieved instead is an industry in touch with present consumers and future consumers.

A factor that today limits the game industry is education. In order to have a wide array of interesting persons to employ in the video game industry there needs to be an educational model that is open to a wider array of persons. Today that is not the case. Education shows sign of reconfirming existing patterns of patterns in society. Breaking these down is a daunting challenge, even for the game industry. Take the example of technology. Although the number of female students in general outnumbers the number of male students at universities, in technical programs male students outnumber female students. This problem is ascribed to the fact that technology is seen as a male province. Technology is for men to tinker with. If technology is constructed for female, it is often takes a simplified form – such as a dishwasher or oven. One button – done! The fact that technology is constructed as a male area of expertise has ripple effects on how girls relate to technology when growing up, forming their interests and making decisions on education and what careers to pursue in life.

The daunting task of creating diversity, we believe, is the primary challenge facing the video game industry. There has been great progress in some areas, but there is still a long way to go in constructing a field that is inclusive and a development process that has the capacity to capture all different kinds of knowledge. The medium itself promises a more diverse market than films, than books – than any other medium to this point. So why are we not seeing this?

On creativity

There is a need to take a long and hard look at the industry when it comes to creativity. We argue that this self-categorization and public categorization do not help the industry, but they could be instrumental in breaking it. If the video game industry in the future is striving to become a place where many different ideas can have their place and a medium that can represent a wide variety of social discourse, we believe that looking critically at what we mean by creativity is a start.

One of the authors once made a public presentation at a video game conference in Paris on the topic of creativity. The presentation was called "There Is No Such Thing as a Creative Industry," and in it I discussed the topic of creativity in the video game industry. You might realize by now that I did not have the audience on my side at the start of this presentation – I did not have them on my side at any time during the presentation, actually. No one likes to hear that he or she is not creative. The point is that the video game industry is not creative per se; no industry or person is! The point is not that there is no creativity in the video game industry but that we reject the idea that there is creativity – all the time. So why would a whole industry claim to be creative?! That is beyond us. We believe that if the video game industry instead embraced the idea of creativity and how that works, then it would have the possibility to apply it better in the future.

There is a much-supported idea that being creative is good. Being creative is something you should achieve. We all like to hear that we are creative. But the point is that none of us is creative all the time. If everything we do is creative, then nothing is creative. The value of creativity finds its meaning in the importance of challenging what we take for granted and what we do every day out of habit. That habitual approach to anything is the essence of being uncreative. A definition of creativity would then involve making familiar things new and challenging our understanding of how things should be done in order to do and think anew. This kind of thinking has proved very efficient in the games industry, from the Doom (id Software) engine to the Sims series (Maxis) of games and micro payments. These have been aspects of game development that have challenged how things are done. There have been moments when the circle of business as usual is suspended, leaving an opening for something new. This, for us, is what being creative is all about.

Claiming that the video game industry is not creative all the time does not render the talented persons in this industry less valuable. We know that there is a huge amount of talent here: coding, graphics, narration, sound, management, marketing and many more skills. We believe that there are opportunities for creative efforts in all these professions. As businesspersons our experience is that there are accountants who are more creative than artists. Notice that this does not say something about values; it just points out that some accountants are proficient at finding ways to account for money. At the same time we know artists who make the most beautiful paintings, but they are not creative. They are artistic, yes. But do they challenge what it means to paint, to use colours, to express emotions? No. They are artistic masters, and therein lies their value.

So creativity is nothing that can define a whole industry. Creativity is not something that can define a whole category of industries – the creative industries. Creativity is a process of critically challenging your knowledge and the practices that you are engaged in to improve and make anew. We do acknowledge that this is indeed part of the video game industry and has been instrumental in transforming the industry. But creativity is not something that defines the whole industry, and it shouldn't!

A large number of activities that you are engaged in daily are habitual and mundane; they are the implementation of something that you do know – and do well. Making Call of Duty: Modern Warfare 3 (Infinity Ward) is not creative. There might be creative aspects to the game, novel features, novel ways for collaboration when making the game. This is great! Previous knowledge brings us yet another game we love from a series of games. That is valuable in itself.

The danger of defining the video game industry as creative is thus the trap of using a self-proclaimed tag that inhibits you from filling "being creative" with any actual content. This is following the logics of "if you already believe you are creative, why prove it?" We believe that the industry has a bright future and can make numerous contributions to consumers. If the industry, the persons working in this industry, is to materialize some of these potential benefits it needs to challenge what it does and how. It is this inability to question what you take for granted that makes your ability to be creative vanish. The value of creativity lies not in its definition but in its application.

Business models

One of the most dominant changes that has taken place in game development over the past five to ten years is in the business models used when developing and delivering games to consumers. Looking back over a longer time than that offers an even greater perspective on how the development of building games and making revenues from games has changed. The start of game development is quite telling here. In an interview with Stephen Kent, Kurt Russell exclaimed that in 1962, when they were finished making Spacewar!, "We thought about trying to make money off it for two or three days but concluded that there wasn't a way that it could be done" (*The Ultimate History of Video Games*, 2001). Today we know it is possible to make money from games – at times, lots of money! But those of you who are trying to make a living by developing games know that most of this money comes hard. How the future of business models is looking is thus the third challenge for the industry. It is not a minor challenge but is the core of survival for the industry.

Again, the changes we are observing in the game industry are not isolated to this industry only. Zooming out, we see that the same problems are also having a major influence on other cultural industries. Unlike film and music, games have effective technical possibilities to protect themselves games from illegal use and copying. From a technical and economical standpoint, this definitely makes things easier. But the video game industry, just like other industries, is dealing with consumers who to a growing degree are finding new ways of consuming – free! This inevitably will affect and already has affected the game industry. How do you convince consumers to spend money for something that they perceive should be free?

The dominant business models today are far more developed and advanced than those of the traditional publishing industry, which was the standard setup in the beginning. The effects of this business model not only are shortening the distance to consumers but also have a far greater impact on the industry. This change presents huge possibilities but also challenges. Some of these challenges we have covered previously when, for example, talking about marketing communication and the importance of finding ways to communicate with consumers. If the publisher is taken out of the distribution from developer to consumer, it then falls back on the developer to establish a channel for communicating with consumers. Business models thus have an effect on economic, cultural and technical aspects of game development.

A business model goes directly to the core of developing games, not only about return on investment but also about how a developer sets up an organization to ensure that the value offered by the games has the biggest impact possible. The challenge is then to develop a business model that both generates profit, and at the same time supports the organization in delivering games that reflect the ambitions of the studio. The challenge might even go further than that. Is it really possible to develop a business model that will sustain your business in the future? We believe that the challenge ahead is to create a model or process in your organization that makes it agile and able to adapt to different business models depending your market.

If the development of micro-transactions, in-game purchases, free to play, and other aspects have taught us something about the video game industry, it is that we can be sure of one thing – things change! This effect is that new technologies mean new possibilities for delivering games in different ways. That is why technology can never be the aim of games but only a platform for delivering games.

Game development thus has to be about finding a platform for delivering games and creating financial possibilities. If game development in the past was all about the game, game development since 2010 needs to be about building a game structure where game and business model work together in order to support a developer's ambitions. The ecology of technological platforms is never stable, and how games are published and how consumers interact with these games on each platform change. Just as technological requirements when building games are part of development, so are business models.

Changes in business models do have an effect on the actual content in games. If consumers are no longer willing to pay money up front for games but instead use micro-transaction for in-game purchases, how can we build the possibility for this to happen into the game? A structure of play-and-pay must then be in place, a structure that supports both play and also pay in order to support the game financially. One way of dealing with this challenge is to change our perception of games, as we suggested in Chapter 3. When games stop being products, when we understand them as services, we can also appreciate games as virtual worlds that contain a number of possibilities for transaction, a service where you can participate in a virtual world and, once there, choose to spend money or stay a visitor.

It's written in the sand

We all know that you are probably as enthusiastic as we are about seeing the development of the video game industry in the years to come. Thus far we have seen a long line of very interesting games and other innovations that have kept us occupied playing. How the industry develops is something that is up to us all – an effect of all the actors developing and playing video games. We are seeing possibilities for video games to take the place as mass media, something that is present in our hands and in our lives on a daily basis. But in order for this medium to reconstruct itself and claim the position of being relevant and inclusive, we believe that the industry needs to continue its work and critically examine what it does, how it does it, and why.

Exercises

1   What are your shared assumptions about games and gaming in your organization, and to what degree do all of you represent different aspects of knowledge and opinions?
2   What can you do in your daily work to challenge your assumptions about how things should be and how things should be done?
3   How much time do you spend designing the business model of your games? Do you exploit possibilities created by technological development to offer your game in improved ways?

Part III
Explore

10 Advergames and in-game advertising

When creating advertising for video games, other cultural industries are often part of the mix. Songs and films are used for creating trailers for games, for example. But games themselves are used as advertising tools for everything from beer to politics because of the messaging value in games. Offering virtual worlds, games are also targeted for advertising for products. This is sometimes understood as part of the game industry and can have a huge impact on developing games.

Learning objectives

1 To understand the relationship among video games, product placement and advertising
2 To understand how product placement and advertising can be part of a strategy for making video games

Today most games use the Internet in creating an online interface, meaning that it constantly communicates with a server at the developer of the game. This feature makes it possible for consumers to play with each other, no matter their geographical location. It also makes it possible for consumers to build and share their own content in the game. It also allows the developer to constantly update the game, by fixing errors (bugs) and improving and introducing new content, and to use these games as a sphere for promotion.

Through different types of in-game advertising, game developers sell advertising spots to third parties, just as in the real world. The idea of promoting brands and products in games is not new in itself; the concept was already present in early soccer games (mimicking the ads displayed on the side of the soccer field). What has changed is the introduction of dynamic in-game advertising, where the ad can be customized to the consumer and third parties. For example, depending on what games you play, a third-party organization can target you as its audience.

There are different ways to introduce ads into games, some of which are copied from your physical setting and some of which are enabled because of the uniqueness of the medium. Among the most common are advertising billboards and product placement. No matter the method used for promotion, the driving philosophy for all games is that the content of the promotion has to be in line with rest of the content of the game. Games are built to form an internal logic, for example, a futuristic world, ancient world, or any other. The promotion then has to add to the content or the suspension of disbelief – immersion – is ruined.

First, games, just like the physical world, can contain billboards. It is possible to display ads on these, as in the physical world. Billboards are used in the same way as in our physical world, as a digital form of billboards in a digital world. Second, just as in film, TV and magazines, video games use product placements. And, just as in these other medium, the products displayed in games must be in line with rest of the content, or the break between the game world and the product will be too great and immersion will be impossible. For example, placing a can of Coca-Cola in a game that uses a medieval setting will break the historical context, although using a bottle of Coca-Cola in a game displaying, for example, New York in the 1950s will only increase the credibility of the game. More than other media, games have a great advantage when using product placement – the gamer can interact with the objects. Drinking a bottle of Coca-Cola in a game can, perhaps, have a greater impact on consumption than watching a person in a film drink one.

Product placement is an adoption from other media. In films it has been used and is still used to such an extent that it has become an industry standard. The difference is that placing products in games not only enables consumers to be visually stimulated by the message but also, and more important, allows gamers to interact with the product in the narrative of the game. There is strong evidence that this seemingly small aspect affects the understanding of the product and inscribes virtual experiences with a feeling of reality, for example, driving cars that have a real-life brand or drinking soft drinks that have a real-life brand.

An interesting contractual phenomenon that has arisen is the relationship between game developers and third-party organizations whose products are promoted in games: who pays whom? As the practice of using promotion is less developed in games than in other media, the question of the relationship is still an open one. If one were to build a racing game, using tracks and cars from the physical world, would the game developer pay the car manufacturers and track owner for the use of their brands, or would the car manufacturers and track owners pay the developers for promoting their brands? This is a question that still seems to be unsolved.

Games as a promotional tool

A last use of video games that seem to be growing is to define the medium itself as a tool for promotion. Whereas the commercial games described earlier are developed in order to communicate one specific message, as the medium itself is neutral, the message can be just about anything: from commercial to political. The impact of these games is in the interactivity they offer. Instead of being a receiver of a message, the gamer is the co-creator of that message in her acts, her interaction with the game.

One could call these types of games Serious Games, games that have purposes other than pure entertainment. This is an umbrella term that includes a number of sub-categories of games with different characteristics, including advergames, edutainment, persuasive games and art games. Although the games have differ-ent goals, be it the communication of knowledge or the presentation of art, they all share the use of doing other things while games do the entertaining. But, here to draw the line between entertainment and its counterpart is sometimes a delicate issue.

One of the most popular Serious Games, although it might not be categorized as such, is America's Army. This is a game funded by the U.S. Army and pub-lished by Ubisoft, a traditional game publisher. The game has been developed specifically to communicate the good life of an American soldier, in order to get more American kids to sign up for the military; a secondary goal to com-municate a positive image of the American soldier abroad. The game is free to play and has more than 8 million registered users.

In the America's Army game, players are bound by Rules of Engagement (ROE) and grow in experience as they navigate challenges in teamwork-based, multiplayer, force-versus-force operations. In the game, as in the army, accom-plishing missions requires a team effort and adherence to the seven Army Core Values. Through its emphasis on team play, the game demonstrates these values of loyalty, duty, respect, selfless service, honor, integrity and personal courage and makes them integral to success in America's Army.

While America's Army is a big production, many companies use smaller games to promote their products or services. These are called advergames. These games usually have a very simple construction. Examples are a three-in-a-row game with Coca-Cola caps and a shoot-'em-up game where you hit Carlsberg bottles with a pistol. These games are spread free over the Internet or played free on the company's homepage. Many times they have a ranking system and prizes for high performers. These games are never long lived as the construction does not offer much game play, although the goal is not game play but getting a consumer to interact with a brand.

There are also advergames with political goals. Games have previously been used in, for example, political campaigns: what better way to explain what the suggested reforms will do for the economy than getting citizens to experience them firsthand through a game? One example of is the game called September 12 (Watercoolergames), which is a contribution to the discussion about terrorism and violence.

The game cannot be won in a traditional sense; rather, it demonstrates the fruitlessness of using violence in a war against terrorism. When players identify the terrorists on the screen and fire a missile on them, there is a delay that kills civilians instead. As one civilian is killed, other gather and mourn, then turn into terrorists. So by interacting with this game, the gamer interacts with a political statement about the physical world.

Exercises

1   What relationships would it be possible to construct for your games? What companies and what products could you link up with?
2   What messages are you today conveying to your customers? What do they learn from playing your games?

11 Gamification

This chapter is about how game mechanisms in non-game contexts, so-called gamification, can be used as a tool for marketing, product/service design and innovation. Gamification is a cutting-edge concept that is relevant to marketing and video games. This chapter introduces a definition of gamification. To understand the background of the gamification trend, we need a historical perspective that traces the roots of the concept in gaming culture and the video game industry. A business case-driven examination of gamification in practice provides us with seven important insights into gamification. These insights are discussed within a broader context to demonstrate the potential of gamification in the future.

Learning objectives

1   To get an introduction to what gamification is
2   To understand the background and theory of gamification
3   To get a breakdown of gamification insights based on real-world business cases and balanced examinations of these claims
4   To get inspiration related to how gamification can be applied to video game development and marketing

Some claim that the term "gamification" was coined as early as 2002 by the game developer Nick Pelling, but the concept has gained attention only more recently. A common yet not universally accepted viewpoint is that gamification involves the use of game mechanisms in non-game contexts. Although lacking in accuracy, this definition has created a global gamification frenzy. A Google Trends query indicates a dramatic surge in the term's popularity at the end of 2010. In 2011 it was termed the hottest digital trend at the immensely influential SXSW festival of digital culture in Austin, Texas. The buzz has inspired a plethora of software applications, services, campaigns, products and communication strategies implemented in an impressing range of fields including weight loss programmes, education, journalism, loyalty programmes, marketing campaigns, exercise, language learning, social networks and corporate intranets.

The gamification trend has primarily been picked up by the IT industry – often entrepreneurial Internet start-ups outside the traditional video game industry. A trailblazer in this context has been the immensely successful case of Foursquare, which, using gamification, has created one of the biggest crowd-sourced local business directories in the world – complete with millions of tips and photos of restaurants, cafés, hotels and other attractions all around the world (including great coffee shop recommendations in Nepal's second biggest city, Pokhara, during a recent trip by one of the authors to the Himalayas). Foursquare is analyzed later, as are other successful cases such as Frequent Flyer Programmes (FFPs), the Nike+ platform and many other interesting cases.

What is gamification?

Although gamification has much older origins, the start of the current wave of gamification is often attributed to the impressive TED talks of Jane McGonigal, Tom Chatfield and Gabe Zichermann in 2010 and 2011. Particularly impressive was the game designer Jane McGonigal's speech, which included a personal story of recovering slowly after an injury and how she used game worlds to fight depression and improve her comeback. Using the principles of so-called positive psychology, she created SuperBetter, a gamified approach to achieving personal growth and tackling real-life challenges, which she claims has helped nearly a half-million people.

The most prominent definition, according to the nascent field of gamification research is this: gamification is the use of game mechanisms in non-game contexts. Clearly, the concept of "game" needs explanation, since it is included three times in this definition. So what is a (video) game in this context? It is important to state at the start that not all games are digital – games include all type of media governed by game mechanisms. A game of chess is a game of chess whether it is played on a physical chess set or on an iPad. To make a long story short, in terms of game research, a game can be define as *a system governed by rules and involving committed players producing uncertain yet categorical results.*

What does this definition entail? First of all, a rule book is needed since games are governed by rules. Every game is governed by rules that regulate what is and what isn't allowed inside the actions of the game. The results of the game are categorical, which means that there are always clear winners and losers. There can be variations of this principle (several winners) – but the point of practically all games is to produce a hierarchical result list. The participants must care about the results; that is, they have to be knowingly committed to the game. There is no such thing as an unaware participant in a game – because otherwise we could all be unaware participants in countless games (e.g. "the game of life", "the market economy game", "the political game of democracy") in which inclusion would rely solely on the definitions of myriad unknown "game makers". Another characteristic is the voluntary link to reality; that is, the game is about play and not about inescapable outcomes such as money or other tangible resources. The difference between a game of poker and gambling is that when the result of a poker game is money profit or loss, this mechanism overshadows the logic of the entire game. Without money results, the game is played for the enjoyment of play, victory and the other usual motivations for playing games. Finally, games are everywhere – they are platform independent and can be played with two hands (rock-paper-scissors) or multimillion-dollar computer systems (war simulation games) – physical medium and representation are irrelevant; game mechanisms are paramount.

So, given this definition of game, where does that leave the previous definition of gamification? An important metaphor here becomes "game machine". The game machine is an imaginary machine that is constituted by the rules of the game. Consequently, games are types of machines that involve players who interact with the machine that defines the possibilities of actions. From a software technological perspective, this metaphor makes more sense for video games since the software is the game machine that allows and manages anything and everything that happens on the screen, including, most important, all the actions of the player. Transferring this metaphor to gamification, we could similarly treat any gamified application as a set of rules that constitute a game machine that defines the possibilities of gamified actions. Consequently, gamification is about applying game rules to non-game applications – in the digital as well as the non-digital realm. In a setting where game rules have not been used previously, such as language-learning software, we apply on top of the software an imaginary layer of rules that stipulate how to gamify this application. These rules can be translated into software, creating a whole new gamified language-learning software (such as Duolingo) – or the rules can remain in the non-digital realm, such as in a classroom where the teacher creates a list of the students who complete the learning assignments in the language learning software the fastest. In the latter case the "application" of language learning in classroom has been gamified with non-digital rules, where as in the case of Duolingo the entire software application has been interwoven with gamified principles written in software.

The obvious question now becomes – why would we gamify something non-game? We all probably know the reasons why we play games, but let us list some of the most popular ones. First of all, games are entertaining – simply put, they are fun. Everyone likes fun – particularly when something arduous is turned into something fun (although some business managers consider "fun" the opposite of "serious" and oppose gamification in professional work settings). Games are fun because they usually give rise to (exciting) experiences for the players – even losing a game can sometimes be a pleasurable experience. For that reason alone it is sometimes worth considering gamification as new perspective on product/service development. These great game experiences are caused by (strong) emotions – from extremely positive to negative and everything in between. Games have an ability to stir up all sorts of emotions, and that is one of the main reasons so many people love them. An illustrative example is sports – the most institutionalized (in terms of status, money, time and dedication) type of game that exists in Western societies. A game of football can cause riots – but it can also bring bursts of euphoria to a stadium full of tens of thousands of fans. Sports-like activities have been part of society as long as civilization has existed. Some even claim that it has existed longer than that – look at kittens (and other animals) playing in order to have fun and also to learn and simulate new behaviour, such as fighting. In short, games create player dedication on multiple layers of entertainment, experiences and emotions, and they are a fundamental part of human existence. Why not make our lives more dedicated through some gamification?

Another way of answering the question "why gamify?" is to take a closer look at how rewards, that is, the results of the game, affect our engagement with the game. A well-known way is to compare intrinsic and extrinsic rewards. Intrinsic rewards are those whose value is understood only within the confines of the game, whereas extrinsic rewards are those whose value is appreciated outside the game as well. Intrinsic rewards are usually symbolic – their meaning and value are created by the game rules and the gamers. A typical example is an impressively high score from a video game. This high score might give a gamer global fame – but only for those who understand the game and the type of effort it takes to achieve this high score. Outside the world of the game, the high score is merely a symbol of something that people don't quite understand or value. Extrinsic rewards are predominantly (although not always) material. Their value can be understood by outsiders since they are things you can touch and things that have values outside the game world. A typical extrinsic award is money. It is material (coins and bank notes), and its value is understood within the economy of that particular currency and in many cases also outside it (via currency exchanges).

Gamification applications predominantly reside in the world of intrinsic rewards – the reward of playing, having fun and being part of a player community, is supposed to be the primary objective of gamification and its participants. But this is not always the case – as we will show, many gamification applications use combinations of intrinsic and extrinsic rewards to stimulate engagement and participation.

History of gamification

In order to understand gamification we need to take a look at the video game industry and gamers, where inevitably gamification has its roots. As mentioned previously in this book, the video game industry is a cultural industry that creates cultural symbols that relate to our social and cultural sensibilities. The previous segment also clarified that (video) games create dedication on many levels.

Video games are not a global mass medium on a par with cinema or music. It may be their equal in terms of revenues and turnaround – but it is not in terms of cultural position. The video game industry is still in many ways a subcultural industry and has been since its dawn. Men and children predominantly play video games, and men utterly dominate the production aspects of video games. Women and seniors (those older than thirty-five or forty years of age) are largely excluded. The aesthetics of the biggest AAA game titles are still what mainstream society would call "unpolished", with gory violence, comics/science-fiction/fantasy-based visuals and excessively epic storylines of good clashing with evil. Content is also often copied or "sequelized" (turned into long series) to such an extent that inexperienced consumers become confused – "what racing game featured that photorealistic red Ferrari Enzo?" The answer, as we all know, is dozens upon dozens of racing titles.

Although all of this is rapidly changing with the arrival of new generations of gamers, game designers and the original gamers are growing much older, and things are still very much stuck in the structures of subcultural dynamics. The GamerGate media scandal and debate (involving issues of sexism, lack of ethics, harassment and political correctness) showed that there is an extremely vocal hardcore group of gamers and game designers who are not interested in evolving the video game culture into a true mass-culture phenomenon and who violently oppose any new perspectives on the video game medium.

One solution for all of these issues that has been raised is the arrival of so-called causal games. These games target a much wider audience, one that includes women and elders. They are much cheaper due to "freemium" business models (play for free, pay for extras) and the fact that they are played on existing equipment (browser, smartphone, tablet, Facebook). Casual games are very often simple, fast and short, such as platform, puzzle and social gaming.

But casual gaming is not without its critics. Some claim it creates a speculation bubble – as illustrated by the case of the casual-game developer Zynga, which skyrocketed on stock exchanges and then almost crashed because of a struggling business model and a lack of new hit titles. Casual gaming audiences are significantly broader than the traditional console-based video game audiences – particularly considering the prevalence of titles such as Angry Birds and Candy Crush Saga Wider – but the question remains whether they are truly mass media. Many of these games represent reinterpretations of old games – Candy Crush Saga is inspired by Bejeweled and other tile-matching video games that have been made since the early 1980s. This gives rise to the obvious question – are casual games the right way forward for the video game medium to move into true mass-media territory?

As it turns out, casual games are not the first attempt to create a truly mass-cultural video game strategy that would be embraced by all of society. There have been several attempts throughout the history of the video game industry. Episodic games (smaller and cheaper games tied together as series) were introduced during the 1980s, portable handheld games (such as Nintendo Game Boy) during the early 1990s. Massive Multiplayer Online Games (MMOGs) were introduced during the late 1990s and revolutionized the game industry with subscription-based business models. After that came the first generation of (predominantly Java-based) mobile games, followed by the arrival of the serious games movements of the early 2000s and then the casual games movement during the late 2000s. All of these strategies attempted to expand the video game medium beyond the confines of the console-based video game market in order to increase market size but also to reposition the video game medium as a truly mass-cultural form of mainstream mass media.

With all of this history in mind, it is obvious that gamification is the next step for turning gaming culture and the video game industry into a mainstream mass-cultural phenomenon. Instead of attempting to convince non-gamers to play video games, it is better to transform non-game contexts into games. Gamification is strongly rooted in the culture of video games and its industry, but, as most cases in this chapter show, the evolution of gamification is driven not by the video game industry but by people outside it.

Hadn't anyone thought of gamification earlier than the 2000s? It turns out that historical research shows that leaderboards (e.g. "employee of the month"), loyalty programs and other marketing-related game elements have been used in marketing and business settings at least since the nineteenth century. It is, in other words, inaccurate to claim that gamification was invented in the 2000s. Game mechanisms in marketing and communications have been around for more than a century, although nobody called them "gamification" and it is only fairly recently that digital media (the preferred medium for gamification) have become mainstream. This older form of gamification was present largely as loyalty schemes or reward programmes, frequency reward programmes, frequent-shopper programmes, loyalty cards or schemes, point cards, advantage cards and frequent flyer programmes – in other words, as fairly widespread marketing strategies that weren't described as games until the gamification trend showed interest for them.

Case: FFPs (frequent flyer programs)

Let us look at the first gamification case – frequent flyer programmes (FFPs). With our historical perspective it is an obvious choice because FFPs are considered the world's biggest gamified service. FFPs were created long before the current gamification craze, in 1981, when American Airlines introduced its AAdvantage FFP (although research has shown that previous similar programmes did exist).

To examine a more contemporary programme we will turn to the airline SAS and its FFP EuroBonus – the biggest FFP in northern Europe, where the authors of this book live. Taken at face value, EuroBonus is yet another rather boring loyalty programme, like any other FFP. But when we take a closer look we discover impressive numbers: it has more than 3 million members, around forty airline partners (in the Star Alliance), about thirty hotel partners, three credit card partners, six taxi and rental car company partners, around twenty other direct partners (e.g. supermarket chains, electricity providers, insurance providers), and finally a Web shop with more than seventy commercial partners offering products and services to the EuroBonus world.

How is the EuroBonus "game" played? There is no cost of entry –every passenger of SAS is frequently prompted to join the FFP. Points – which are part of every FFP – are earned by flying with SAS or its airline partners and buying products at any of its hundreds of partners. Points can also be bought – indicating clearly that EuroBonus points are a type of virtual currency. Optionally points can also be won with associated credit cards –points are collected for every transaction (regardless of where it is done). Points are meant to be spent on free or discounted products or services with all of the EuroBonus partners but are used most efficiently in exchange for SAS travel services. There four different user ("game") levels: Member, Silver, Gold and Diamond, and each is associated with a different set of points, offers, rewards and services.

The question now becomes: can FFPs be considered games? All the characteristics of our previously discussed game definition apply (possibly with slight ambiguity with regard to the involuntary link to outcomes – FFPs sometimes involve substantial expenses and savings). The game's point system is a type of virtual currency used predominantly within the game world (EuroBonus points are meant to be spent on SAS flights). As a new member/player, you are offered "qualifying flights" by the EuroBonus system; that is, you get fast bonus-point earnings that provide instant gratification, like game designs where beginners are drawn into the game through an easy intro level or a quick upgrade. Similarly, FFPs make use of "points campaigns" – strategies to make players spend points on targeted campaigns (e.g. a new flight destination). This resembles certain video games that seek to "balance" excessive point accounts (e.g. in the Ratchet & Clank series, a lot of points can be spent on special gold versions of weapons that have no apparent difference from other weapons except that they are made of virtual gold). A final similarity between FFPs and games is the use of progression levels or difficulty levels. In FFPs this is represented by different cards (in the EuroBonus case there are four levels – although a mysterious fifth superlevel has been secretly confirmed to exist). Depending on the airline, FFP and market, these different levels offer several classes of rewards, such as priority check-in, priority boarding, priority security check, separate airport entrances, airport lounges, free upgrades to better classes of seats, better in-flight meals and free taxi transportation to hotels.

The similarities between FFPs and games definitely qualify FFPs as games, and FFPs can therefore be considered one of the most successful implementations (in terms of active users) of gamification techniques in the world. The next question is: why do airlines create FFPs? Airlines, according to research (which has been questioned) believe FFPs reduce customer acquisition costs due to increased consumer loyalty, as well as network effects – FFP members spread the word about the airline and its offerings. Consumers see predominantly economic benefits by earning discounts through FFPs. From an airline's perspective, FFPs provide low-cost bonuses – upgrades to higher levels mainly consist of symbolic benefits such as different FFP cards, access to airport lounges, and priority boarding – nothing that really adds to fixed costs (having an airport lounge or managing a priority boarding queue on every flight). These bonuses provide significant symbolic status for certain consumers – getting VIP treatment indicates substantial prestige for many consumers (although for many it is hard to admit to this). For airlines, FFPs offer a strategic marketing tool that can be used to manage relationships with their top clients, the frequent flyers, and to create direct communication with different segments of frequent flyers. For consumers there is a minimal, yet tangible, experience of game play when earning points and in particular when getting an upgrade to the next level of the FFP. All of this is based primarily on intrinsic rewards but carries a touch of extrinsic rewards (bigger baggage allowance, more point earnings, more discounts and other economic-like benefits).

Case: offline gamification

The FFP case illustrates a fairly obvious point – that digital media are not needed to implement a successful gamification application. FFPs were created long before the introduction of the first PCs and long before the Internet, social media and mobile computing. Another successful offline gamification example is My Coke Awards by Coca-Cola in the United States. It is based on earning points on special codes on the inside of Coca-Cola bottle caps, which are then registered by text message or entered on a Web page. Although quite different from FFPs, this program uses the same underlying game logic – to reward top consumers through a loyalty programme where the collected My Coke Rewards can be used to acquire products and services from more than forty programme partners.

The cases of FFPs and My Coke Rewards help us arrive to the first gamification insight:

Insight: gamification can be non-digital and has been for many years.

Although practically all current gamification applications rely on a digital component, many of the same applications can be successfully implemented using non-digital offline tools. Gamification does not have to be digital.

Case: Foursquare

As mentioned in the introduction, a pioneer of the gamification trend is the strikingly thriving app Foursquare, a location-based social network for smartphone users. In many ways it has been, in the eyes of the IT industry, media and, to some extent, researchers, the "face of gamification" since its outset. It was founded in 2009 and since then has grown to 55 million users with 7 billion so-called check-ins and 70 million user tips. Unlike many new social media platforms, Foursquare remains an independent start-up company, and its user growth is self-made without the backing of financial and infrastructural support from the major Internet giants such as Google, Facebook, Twitter, Microsoft, Yahoo and Amazon.

Foursquare competes in a crowded market with other hugely popular "recommendation systems" for local businesses such as Google Maps (all businesses), Yelp (all businesses with consumer focus), TripAdvisor (travel-related businesses), Zomato (food-related business), Zagat (food-related business), Foodspotting (food-related business), Yellow Pages (all type of businesses) and Qype (all businesses with consumer focus). In 2014 the service was split into two apps – Foursquare and Swarm. Foursquare focused on discovery and recommendations of local businesses, whereas Swarm focused on social networking, check-ins and chat.

So what is a "check-in"? When you physically enter a local business, you "check in" with the Foursquare/Swarm app by pressing a button and announcing your geographical location to everyone in your friend list. You can leave comments, and the app(s) prompts you to write a "tip" (short recommendation), evaluate various aspects of the business or upload a photo. All of this is aggregated, analyzed and ranked by Foursquare's servers, which later, using actual check-ins (geographically verified), rank the popularity of a given place. This gives Foursquare a distinct advantage over other recommendation services, which are based on anonymous user recommendations, making them more vulnerable to rating manipulations.

When you check in frequently to a place, you are awarded various badges (e.g. a "Joey beans" badge when you check in often to cafés and coffee bars), and if you check in to a certain place more frequently than anyone else during a period, you become "the Mayor" of that place. Others (non-friends or friends) can reclaim that position by checking in more times during the next period. This creates a competitive element. The badge and mayor system has been extensively modified over the years, but at the core it is a competitive game of badges and mayorships by means of the check-in mechanism.

So, why these badges and mayorships? They are a "symbolic medal of achievement" and constitute a classic case of intrinsic rewards – you can be the Foursquare mayor of the Eiffel Tower, but most of the external non-Foursquare world doesn't even understand what it means. There is basically no cost associated with badges and mayorships – they are game principles transformed into software by Foursquare's programmers. It is a case of artificial scarcity that increases demand – a classic principle of luxury consumer goods economics: the harder to get and the rarer a product is, the more it generates interest among potential consumers. Badges and mayorships are gamification in a nutshell – influencing human behaviour with symbolic/ intrinsic rewards, and they constitute Foursquare's/Swarm's globally successful implementation of gamification principles.

But, what is so impressive about Foursquare besides making check-ins into a game? Simply put, Foursquare has managed to successfully gamify information crowdsourcing for one of the world's biggest local business databases. Maintaining an updated local business database requires a lot of resources and effort. Crowdsourcing is a risky solution since it is hard to manage for a number of reasons: the risk of manipulation, the use of free work, copyright and commercialization/ownership by a company (Foursquare) of others' altruistic work. By gamifying crowdsourcing activity (check-ins, badges and mayorships), ratings and recommendations, Foursquare has cleverly created a vibrant crowdsourcing community – one that most likely isn't even aware of the fact that it is providing valuable information; for example check-ins are used to determine opening hours and customer retention by permitting the intelligent analysis of user data. There is also a top layer of superusers that administer new/double entries, disputes and abuses. This leads us to another gamification insight:

> *Insight: gamification can make trivial activities exciting.*

And the Foursquare case provides us with a bonus insight:

> *Insight: rewards, such as badges and points, are currently some of the most popular gamification mechanisms.*

Case: gamification as motivator

The case of Foursquare indicates that certain difficult tasks – such as creating a thriving crowdsourcing community – can be facilitated by good gamification design. Others have taken this message to heart and searched for new areas where gamification can affect behaviour. One fundamental idea that comes into mind is our daily grind of chores – something that a sea of to-do apps has addressed in countless ways. Some developers of apps such as EpicWin, Todoist Karma and HabitRPG think gamification might be a winning strategy for getting things done, and they have combined game aesthetics and mechanisms with to-do apps. In these apps, intrinsic rewards, such as badges, animations, sound effects and even role-playing characters, are used as mechanisms to grease the wheels of activity and diligence. Competing against yourself and against others is a central gamification strategy in these apps.

Another applicable common area of many lives is workout. Services such as Keas and Fitocracy have gamified workout motivation apps. Keas is a community-based gamified health service system for corporations that engage their employees, whereas Fitocracy is combining a social network approach with gamification elements based on intrinsic rewards and competitions. This provides another insight:

> *Insight: gamification can motivate people to overcome challenges by generating dedication and interest through the use of competitive mechanisms.*

Case: generating communities and product platforms with gamification

Many gamification applications, particularly those geared toward consumers, use gamification in symbiosis with communities; Foursquare, Keas and Fitocracy all use gamification as part of social networks. As the previous insight indicated, competitive game mechanisms are improved by communities, since they supply new competitors and consequently also stimulate activity. A gamification application that has developed this line of thinking is the Swedish energy giant

Vattenfall's smartphone app King of the Slope, created to highlight the company's long-standing sponsorship of winter sports and the Swedish Ski Association. Using geo-location features of smartphones, the app verifies and measures the time it takes to ski down a slope. Then, using a community in combination with gamification mechanisms based on competition and intrinsic rewards, the app allows users to become the fastest "king" of the slopes. Without the competitive community, users would have to compete only against themselves, transforming the app into merely a type of timer.

A company that has taken competitive game mechanisms, combined them with a community and created an entire product category around this is Nike, with its Nike+ platform. The platform began as a small sensor that could be fitted on special Nike+ running shoes. The collected running data were transmitted via a special wireless receiver to the iPod Nano, the best-selling music device in the world at the time, which could be connected via a USB cable to Mac/iTunes software and uploads to the Nike+ online community. Nike then made a standalone Sportband (connected to the Nike+ sensor and Nike+ online uploading via USB), a GPS sportwatch (built-in Nike+ sensor and Nike+ online uploading via USB); later, Apple's smartphones directly communicated with the Nike+ sensor and Nike+ online or via the Nike+ GPS smartphone app (omitting the need for sensors). Finally, Nike released a wristband called Nike+ FuelBand, which, using a proprietary measurement unit called "NikeFuel", measures the user's physical activity and, via smartphone, uploads to the Nike+ online community. The user's current NikeFuel count is shown on a small display, creating a competitive game mechanism through which users can compare NikeFuel status in the real world or online.

The driving force behind the entire Nike+ platform is the plan to upload activity data to the Nike+ community, where real competitors/users, competitive game mechanisms, badges and a thriving community enrich the entire platform. Without the online community, the Nike+ platform would be an activity tracking technology, but with the gamified online community the technology is transformed into an ecosystem of connected products – a product platform. A concluding insight becomes:

> *Insight: gamification can facilitate community activities and entire product platforms based around them.*

Case: social media as gamification

Social media might not be perceived as "games", but if we take a closer look we can discover several gaming mechanisms at the very core of most social media platforms. Foursquare/Swarm has a very prominent gamification design visible to the users of its social network, where every check-in results in points and badges and mayorships are prominently displayed at almost every check-in and on user profile pages. Most other networks, such as Facebook, Twitter, Instagram, Snapchat and Tumblr, have no explicit gamification design philosophy, but it is definitely integrated even if in a very discreet fashion. Most social networks do provide so-called metrics directly to the user – how many users are requesting to become your friends, how many friends the user has in total, how many likes the user's posts received, how many comments, how many shares, how many followers and many other statistics. These have become standard features of social networks and are taken for granted but are by no inherently logical – why should we as users be bombarded with all these statistics? The answer might lie in competitive gamification mechanisms. If social networks quantify all our social network actions, then comparison between different actions becomes a given consequence. Most users would agree that a post with a lot of comments and likes from friends does make you reflect on the reasons behind all of that confirmation. Some would even say that this makes some users proud, happy and satisfied – even if only for a few minutes. Many of us would even claim that everyone surely has someone in his or her friend list who is actively (or subconsciously) looking for as many likes and comments as possible – searching for approval and popularity. All these metrics trigger the competitive spirit among many users. It definitely triggers design strategies on social networks – most social networks currently have algorithms that select the most popular articles and friend posts and recommended company pages on the basis of metrics. All users are, in other words, seeing a social media feed shaped by competitive selection made by server algorithms.

The question becomes whether all these metrics are just statistical observations or mechanisms of systematized victory bragging. Let us analyze this issue by looking at intrinsic rewards such as badges or points. These are types of medals, which inevitably are a distinguishing reward. Hierarchy is the foundation of rewards – not everyone can win, and frequently only one person can – so a very small percentage of participants will become winners (hence the allure of the badges to many people). A hierarchy is based on selective mechanisms that define the rules of who becomes a winner and who doesn't. In the case of a game, these are constituted by many (but not all) game rules. Hierarchies of selective mechanisms generate competitions; not everyone wants to participate, but a lot of people are drawn to competitions. These are considerations worthy of game philosophy, but, inevitably, competitively disposed people enjoy the contest because it is a quest for action, survival, affirmation and exceptional focus. With this line of reasoning we have shown how "innocent" statistical observations can act as rewards that generate hierarchies of selections, giving rise to the competitions and contests that constitute games. In other words, social networks rely extensively on gamification by triggering competitive inclinations of participants. This leads to yet another gamification insight:

Insight: social media are based on gamification mechanisms such as competition and rewards.

Case: gamification as marketing communications

Since this is book about video game marketing, it would be prudent to include cases of marketing gamification. This is more difficult than it seems, since this book takes a broader view of marketing, seeing it as a long process that starts before the product or service is created and finishes long after the consumer has bought it. Marketing is, in other words, something more than advertising. Unfortunately, there are currently very few companies or organizations that include gamification as part of a long-term strategic marketing process. Gamification is instead involved during the later stages of the marketing process.

Nonetheless, the hybrid field of marketing communications deals with the dimension of communication with a market(s). This is also not limited to advertising, sales and promotion (but does prominently include them); it also involves all types of communication efforts associated with the entire marketing process. Examples of gamification in this subfield or hybrid field are more frequent.

A perfect examples is "Gaming for Good," by Al Gore's Climate Reality Project, in which gamification was used as a communication platform for information about the climate threat. The Climate Reality Project organized a developer contest open to the public but geared toward communication/digital agencies to come up with the best prototype for a gamified information campaign about the climate threat. Numerous projects were presented, ranging from video game mod(ification)s to GPS-based carbon foot print trackers combined with social networks to competitive e-learning applications. Gamification was not at the core of the Climate Reality Project's entire "marketing" (in this case, education campaign), but it was definitely used as a type of marketing communications platform to reach out to as many people as possible.

An illustrative but purely commercial gamification-based case of marketing communications is Thefuntheory.com, which was a wide-ranging set of Volkswagen campaigns that focused on fun and playfulness. A specific campaign called the "Speeding Lottery" relied heavily on gamification. Simply put, it involved the gamification of "legal driving" by scanning the registration plates of all moving cars on a street in Stockholm, Sweden. All cars that were moving within the legal speed limit automatically joined a lottery whose prize money came from the fines paid by drivers who had been ticketed for speeding on that particular street. This introduced a gamification mechanism that premiered, in a way, legal driving. This gamified communication campaign generated so much attention that the Swedish National Society for Road Safety (which cooperated with VW on the campaign) proposed that the gamification system be introduced on a national level. The stated purpose of the communication campaign was to draw attention to legal driving but also to promote fun solutions to societal challenges ("The Fun Theory"). All of this had an assumed goal of associating the VW brand with fun, playfulness, road safety and innovative thinking.

A final successful case of marketing communication gamification campaign is the "MINI Getaway", a celebrated smartphone app–based marketing communications campaign in which users were physically hunting a virtual MINI car on the streets of real cities with the help of maps inside the app. The person who occupied the virtual car at a given end-time would win the car's real-world equivalent. There were also game mechanisms in place that allowed drivers to poach the virtual MINI car from another participant. This was an allusion to the mass-cultural heritage of the MINI car and the 1960s cult movie *The Italian Job*, in which MINI cars were featured prominently as escape vehicles for bank robbers. The marketing communication campaign received several awards and, after its initial run in Stockholm, Sweden, was repeated in Copenhagen, Denmark, and Tokyo, Japan.

The Climate Reality Project, The Fun Theory and the MINI Getaway campaign produce the final gamification insight:

> *Insight: gamification is not only a product/service innovation philosophy; it is also an efficient communication platform that can be used for marketing and marketing communications.*

Analysis of gamification insights

To conclude the gamification cases and the insights they yield: gamification is the use of game mechanisms in non-game contexts.

Let us review all of the insights accumulated from the gamification cases:

1   *Gamification can be non-digital and has been for many years.*
2   *Gamification can make trivial activities exciting.*
3   *Rewards, such as badges and points, are currently some of the most popular gamification mechanisms.*
4   *Gamification can motivate people to overcome challenges by generating dedication and interest through the use of competitive mechanisms.*
5   *Gamification can facilitate community activities and entire product platforms based around them.*
6   *Social media is based on gamification mechanisms such as competition and rewards.*
7   *Gamification is not only a product/service innovation philosophy; it is also an efficient communication platform that can be used for marketing and marketing communications.*

These insights paint a fairly rosy picture indeed of what gamification is all about. To provide a more nuanced understanding of gamification, we need to examine some critical perspectives. First we turn to criticism from a practitioner point of view, and then we look at research perspectives. It is important to remember that criticism complements previous claims; it does not invalidate them. In other words, both perspectives can be correct, and both provide a deeper understanding of gamification as a concept.

The first practical criticism is that gamification is merely a fad that will disappear when the novelty wears off. Gamification is indeed a very hot buzzword that has made the trend charts of (digital) media, PR, advertising and the IT industries for several years. A fad is usually something short-lived and shallow in its consequences. This leads to the second criticism: that gamification is a simplistic recipe for (digital) success, frequently in management or corporate settings. Undeniably, gamification has been applied in all sorts of uncritical ways and to areas that are not always suitable for gamification strategies. Consultants stand to make a lot of money by claiming to be able to quickly solve many crucial challenges facing marketing, media and management, such as user engagement, user retention and community activity, by transforming the trivial into fun and increasing playfulness in the work life. Not surprisingly, they tend to emphasize the benefits of gamification. Particularly questionable in the eyes of critics is the "badgification" of everything. Gamification is quite often simplistically reduced to the introduction of badges to any challenging task, in the hope that this will make users happier and more engaged. Do intrinsic rewards really solve any complex challenges?

These are all very valid criticisms of the gamification trend. The concept has been excessively hyped, almost to the point of ridicule, and this affects judgements of the entire phenomenon. The hype will inevitably disappear, as it always does, and Google Trends may be indicating that this is already happening, since the word "gamification" reached its popularity peak in 2014 and dropped off 2015. Despite this development, we must separate the reputation of gamification in business from the validity of the central core concept – to apply game mechanisms in non-game contexts – and this is a long-term trend regardless whether it is called "gamification" or something else. Gamification does not solve everything, and it is definitely healthy that expectations be adjusted to more reasonable levels. But how do we adjust these expectations? We turn to research perspectives to find out some more.

Analysis of research perspectives

Research perspectives are based on the work of gamification researchers and also that of theorists from game studies, game philosophy and other relevant close areas. One of these perspectives relates gamification to game archetypes. The French game theorist Roger Caillois once famously categorized all games into four types: competition (*agon*), games of chance/luck (*alea*), role playing (*mimesis*) and vertigo (*ilinx*, or changing the perception of senses). We can see a lot of interesting similarities between these types and gamification. Role playing is used in some gamification cases (e.g. HabitRPG, EpicWin, social media), as are games of chance/luck (e.g. Speed Lottery). Vertigo is not a factor in any of the cases and is rarely used at all in gamification applications. Competition is the most interesting category, since it is present in all of the cases, and when we survey gamification applications more broadly we find that the same pattern applies – competitive game mechanisms are very popular in gamification. As a result we can understand gamification as something that frequently taps into the competitive spirit of its participants. Many participants are not even aware of their competitive nature, particularly in the case of social media. The discussion around social media in research has focused extensively on how to build communities and optimize audience attention and on role playing in social media. A common theme is to discuss the "digital personas" that people construct through social media and how they diverge from and converge with the perceived realities of its users. This aspect falls into the category of role playing/mimesis – we imitate and reproduce certain (created) roles by means of social media.

This is all fascinating, but we would like to turn our attention to the competitive (*agon*) dimension of social media, since this is a less explored perspective. As discussed in the segment about social media above, competitive gamification mechanisms are inherently part of nearly all social media platforms. The competitive dimensions of social media community are triggered as soon as the platform starts comparing members' activity via statistics and metrics. This is a very powerful yet delicate force – selection mechanisms, hierarchy and rewards can, if not managed correctly, turn into mechanisms of exclusion and injustice. A speculative hypothesis is that this might contribute to an explanation for why social media networks such as Facebook generate aversion among many groups of experienced users – they have grown tired of all the superficial bragging by competitive Facebook members and the feelings of exclusion that the Facebook community generates (there are many other factors that contribute to this development).

This last example indicates that game mechanisms are more prevalent than expected. Many researchers claim that gamification is now expanding into nearly all types of new/digital media. This is part of a much wider trend over the past several decades – one that we can call the "media society", in which media start mimicking other media and society starts adapting to media logic. In the media society film originally mimicked theatre, radio mimicked lectures and speeches, video games mimic film (and almost everything else!) – and all types of digital media (regardless of type of application) are mimicking (video) games. This last process, the mimicking of games, is what we have discussed in this chapter as gamification – but it might be also seen in the bigger picture of Western societies becoming more and more influenced by the popularity and expansion of media in society. In other words, gamification is an element of the "media society" – the "mediatization" of society and culture. Gamification is merely the earliest name of the latest iteration of a much larger tendency in societies with mass-media forms. Game mechanisms will continue to experiment and grow in society and create new forms of hybrid trends.

Analysis of critical perspectives

Now let us use these insights from practical and research perspectives and analyze them with critically constructive perspectives.

Gamification is bigger than we might think, and it is growing. It is also increasing competitiveness in the media society. Doesn't all of this sound slightly scary? Are we supposed to happily compete over and play in relation to everything in the gamified society of the future? Is the future of society a competitive "game" in which all the individual benefits gained from society are seen as "game rewards"? The question becomes this: in evil gamification, who's playing what and whom? There are a lot of researchers who share this view and warn us of "evil gamification". Gamification is sometimes in these debates called "Viagra for engagement dysfunction", "chocolate-covered broccoli" or "exploitationware" in which participants are seen as "playborers" (i.e. combination of players and laborers). Basically, it is claimed that gamification is practically always used as a "playful smokescreen" to manipulate people into doing something they don't want to do by other people who seem to gain by this exploitation. Simply put, maybe there is a solid reason why things are not fun, and gamification cannot change this, although it may distract us slightly. Putting badges on tax returns will not make paying taxes more fun or engaging. These limitations of gamification are self-evident, but more intriguing is the presentation of something neutral, objective and without an agenda. Like all media technologies, gamification is not inherently good or bad; it merely exists as a tool for media distribution. Despite this claim, there must be an understanding that someone is using this tool and that this someone is not as neutral as the technology – because after all it is a human, an organization or a company with a certain agenda. Therefore, gamification cannot be seen as a technology/strategy/process that drives "good" wherever it is applied. As several researchers have pointed out, gamification can easily be used for "bad" purposes, including exploitation, surveillance, micro-management, coercion under the guise of obligatory "fun", and other forms of managerial abuse. Some researchers would even go so far as to claim that practically all cases of gamification are abuses – Foursquare is gamified surveillance and monetization of user activity data, FFPs are mechanisms of hierarchical exclusion, and gamified marketing communication campaigns are merely fun distractions that expose potential customers to commercial propaganda (i.e. advertising/promotion).

An alternative research perspective that counters this rather dismal analysis of the future of gamification is moving forward by focusing on gameplay and competition. We should avoid creating manipulative gamification and instead focus on incorporating the joy of playing games and of competition, which is a fundamental characteristic of almost all societies in the world. Competitive spirit can be a source of very positive change; many great leaders of change had competitive personalities. Some game philosophers claim that competition is older than human culture and that it has always accompanied societies since the dawn of civilization. Having said this, there are perils with this alternative perspective of "playful competition", since humans are more complex beings than "competitive animals" who don't question the rules. Some researchers envision a future where good-hearted legislators will "nudge" the rules of games to influence our societies into behaving "the right way". As stated earlier, this would force us to examine the agendas of legislators, since as humans they are not as "neutral" and "fun" as the tools of gamification. In the end, a future in which our goodhearted leaders "nudge" us into good behavior through gamification is probably a more compelling vision of the future than a society where the same leaders strong-arm us into obedience.

Exercises

1   Applying gamification to video games might seem a redundant, round-about of a concept – but consider how game mechanisms from your game design could be incorporated into your marketing (communications) strategy. Do you see any parallels?

2   Find and analyze a famous real-world gamification case in the video game industry. What are its key success factors?

3   What kind of game mechanisms are most popular in gamification applications? And what other, less explored, mechanisms do you think could be implemented in gamification?

12 Alternate reality games

Games and game structure can be used in settings other than the physical game. Games are very effective as promotional tools. Alternate Reality Games have been used on several occasions to promote products, even video games. As such it they are powerful tools that encourage the consumer to take part in the product experience at an early stage.

Learning objectives

1   To describe Alternate Reality Games and how they have been employed in promoting products
2   To learn about the impact of Alternate Reality Games on the video game industry
3   To learn how to apply the lessons learned in building Alternate Reality Games to other types of game development

Games have been used through history in many different settings and for many different reasons, from using chess to learn battleground strategies to iPad applications for learning math. Alternate Reality Games (ARGs) are a form of network narrative that utilizes several different media to engage gamers and create a highly immersive setting. Narratives that spanned several media were used before ARGs offered a possibility to utilize digital media and physical media in areas where they both created individual strength and complemented each other in tying these media together. The first ARGs were first launched in the 1980s with the help of BBS technology, but it was not until the end of the 1990s, or early 2000, that this way of engaging narratives reached bigger audiences. It was also at this point that Jane McGonigal and other academics started to notice the value of these highly engaging narratives.

ARGs are foremost games – very engaging games that have a lot to offer to the gamer and that we think have only started to show their value. The reason we choose to include ARGs in this book about marketing is that as a tool for marketing they resonate both with what the game industry is developing and with the audience that is playing games. There are different types of ARGs: educational, serious, persistent world and so on. But there are also those that are built in order to communicate a message to the consumers – as tools for marketing communication. We believe that the video game industry has great potential for exploring ARGs as an effective interactive tool for market communication because of the seemingly nice fit.

The benefit with using ARGs in market communication is that they engage and involve the consumer with whom you want to communicate. This not only enables you to communicate about your game or any other product but also creates a buzz about your games and starts building a community toward whom you can direct your communication. There is a saying that the golden rule of used-car salesmen is to get the hesitant consumer to sit in the car, to drive the car. Once that individual has sat in the car and felt its steering wheel, the power of acceleration, or the comfort in the design, it is easier to close the deal. In a way, we would like to suggest that ARGs are not only a communication tool but also a possibility to offer the consumer a way to try out the narrative of whatever game you are building. More about that later when we describe three different ARGs that have been used to promote products.

So, what then is an Alternate Reality Game? Basically it is a narrative that is played out on different platforms. The game is designed for the hive mind, for gamers to collectively engage in the challenges and obstacles presented. We have very little insight into the design of the game or its progress, as one of the main design philosophies is a "this is not a game" (TINAG) aesthetic. As will become evident later, if an ARG is understood not as a game but as a mystery or something strange, the design has been successful. The actual design and performance are orchestrated by a puppet master, just as in any tabletop game. Using only small queues, the narrative of the games is presented for the hive mind to find and explore.

One way we have found it helpful to describe an ARG is by comparing it to the 1997 move *The Game* with Michael Douglas. the movie's plot reads this way: "Wealthy San Francisco financier Nicholas Van Orton gets a strange birthday present from wayward brother Conrad: a live-action game that consumes his life." What is evident in this movie is how a dense narrative that is well orchestrated does have the possibility to create a layer of reality and to truly become an alternate reality. The key characteristics are present: TINAG, puppet masters, and different platforms. On one way, however, the examples are not identical, as the reality presented to Nicholas Van Orton is directed not to a hive mind but only to a single person who has no idea what he is up against.

Quite a few successful ARGs have launched since early 2000. We have selected three of these to present here: The Beast, I Love Bees and The Art of the Heist. All of these have ingredients that we believe have the potential of communicating both how a successful ARG can be designed and also how ARGs can be used as a tool for market communication that strengthens the interaction with consumers.

The Beast

When the movie *A.I.: Artificial Intelligence* was being launched in 2001, an ARG was created to promote the film. This seems to be one of the first instances where ARGs were used as a promotional tool. Maybe it was the theme of the move, artificial intelligence in the form of a young boy, that created a good fit for an ARG. There were also plans to release a series of Microsoft games based on the same theme, the same IP. In line with the narrative of the film, Sean Stewart and Pete Fenlon were assigned to create a narrative and a multi-platform world that could host this game. The magazine *Internet Life* wrote about the ARG as a "runaway success" with more than 3 million users. Although the game initially was known by other names, ending up with an asset list of 666 items, it was soon named The Beast.

The Beast ran only for three month, and never during this time was the game advertised. No rules were ever published, and it was never admitted that the game even existed. This is all in line with the TINAG aesthetics.

After having noticed some strange clues online, Cabel Sasser started the Cloudmaker group in April 2001. This was the first organizing effort of the hive mind. Just like Cabel, thousands of persons had noticed strange things that seemed to surround the upcoming movie *A.I.*, for example a credit in a trailer to "Jeanine Salla, Sentient Machine Therapist". This and many other clues were the result of a design that included a large number of Web pages.

As the hive mind started to untangle the network of digital and physical clues, it created a community of highly dedicated persons who invested much time and effort to solve the mysteries that were uncovered. Whatever the hive mind found was shared on different forums.

The narrative that was uncovered was vast. It contained three major mysteries all tangled into several rich sub-narratives that supported one another and led the hive mind forward and into dead ends. Nearly four thousand texts, videos and images distributed over the Web as clues for the hive mind to find. And it found most of these clues.

A hive mind works extraordinary well in solving puzzles. The designer had built several puzzles with the purpose of presenting huge challenges that would require the collaboration of a huge number of persons and take weeks to solve – only to find that they were solved in days.

The Beast thus presented a number of clues for the hive mind to find. These led to challenges to be solved. Bit by bit, the narrative that was set in the year of 2141 was unveiled. In line with the different platforms, the clues were also physical: phone calls, faxes, television, ads in newspapers and even scribbling on public walls in Chicago, New York and Los Angeles. The hive mind that engaged in solving the mysteries thus had to engage with a physical setting.

The developer of The Beast never admitted it was a game. At some point the puppet masters of the game had to stop supporting the game and presenting more challenges or clues. At this point it became evident how much the ARG had meant to many of the participants, as the community continued looking for clues and pieces to the puzzle for another two months. The game thus started through small clues in order to draw people into the narrative that had been constructed, but it also ended in silence – fading away, not revealing the origin of what had taken place. The silence played a big part in creating the success, as it transferred the power to the consumer to discover the narrative and in the end made no effort in diminishing their efforts by exposing the highly designed structure.

It is in the interest of an ARG to present itself as an Alternate, as being yet another dimension of reality. Any efforts that are made to connect the game to a reality will destroy the suspension of disbelief, the willingness of the persons involved to set aside scepticism and reality in order to immerse themselves in the fantasy that is presented. It was only through building on that same narrative as the movie *A.I.* that The Beast could be connected to it as a promotion effort, although the success of The Beast was most likely due to the fact that it was understood not as promotion but as a mystery to be engaged in.

The Beast shows what is possible to do when it comes to engaging consumers in your market communication. If the takeaway from Chapter 5 was that effective market communication is dependent on engaging consumers, this was truly what happened here. Creating an ARG does require much effort and planning if it is to work properly. It is a lot to demand of any game developer to engage in these efforts to promote a game – almost creating yet another game to promote the game.

We believe there are two learning outcomes from this. One is that there are structures of ARGs that can be applied successfully; their design philosophy and interactivity will create strong platforms for communicating with customers. The second outcome goes beyond mere promotion, given the success of ARGs, and asks whether there are ways to incorporate these elements into game design. Both of these aspects will change how you view promotion and game design if employed fully.

I Love Bees

I Love Bees (ILB) was launched in 2004 to promote the video game Halo 4, developed by Bungie. Much of the structure that had been in place for The Beast was repeated for ILB. And indeed, many developers who had been commissioned for The Beast also worked on ILB. This was one of the first ARGs used to promote a video game.

Just as in the case of The Beast, what sparked the game was a clue left in the trailer of Halo 4, a clue that led to a Web page that seemed to have been hacked by some form of intellectual being. What soon became clear was that this was a narrative about an alien artificial intelligence that was trapped on Earth and had found a temporary home in our digital highways.

Just as in its predecessor The Beast, I Love Bees used both online and offline sources to drive the story forward. Having learned from what happened the last time, the hive mind was challenged. The developers knew the power that was able to come together when thousands of persons decide to solve a problem. But, unlike with The Beast, they managed to create an ARG that drove people together in a physical setting by exposing the hive mind to different challenges that would lead to a GPS position and setting a time for hundreds of people to meet at these spots, a pay phone that would ring at that specific time, with the voice of an actor giving clues that would lead the hive forward.

Just like The Beast, I Love Bees was about creating an adventure to be engaged in without writing in big advertising letters "COME PLAY". This was another game that let people find the game and be exposed to the hive mind in solving the challenges and puzzles presented to them.

The Art of the Heist

The last example is from an industry that is not about narratives. This is interesting because even without that element it show the possibilities of ARGs, not only as a promotional tool for the cultural industries but also as a promotional tool to be used for consumers enthralled by games and playing.

In 2005 the car manufacturer Audi brought its new model A3 to the United States to be displayed at different car shows around the country. But, after only a few stops the organizers reported that the car had been stolen. A few days later a video also appeared that seemed to show two persons smashing a window at a car dealership, breaking in and stealing the car. There was an announcement that the public should keep its eyes open for an A3 that was being driven around. As there were not many A3s in the United States at that point, it would not be hard to spot. And did people get engaged! There were messages of the A3 being spotted all around the country by car owners who were engaged in spotting the A3 and sharing information about its whereabouts. But then there were the car shows. Audi had a full booth, all but the car. There were salespersons doing their best to promote a car they could not show except in pictures and on film.

It was all a game. Of course the car was not stolen. Once the car had been removed from that car dealership, a large number of A3s were spotted being driven around, and drivers reported on their sightings. Thus consumers remained involved, driving the plot forward. The actors at the car shows also played their parts well, sometimes appearing really upset because they had no car to display and therefore building on the story of the ARG.

What was interesting about this ARG is the fact that it went beyond cultural goods. The Art of the Heist showed the great potential in using puzzles that engage consumers. But the narrative was not unfolding as the hive mind solved online puzzles as the previous examples but involved people physically as spotters. This offers just a glimpse of what can be done.

Generating audiences

When you use an ARG to promote a game, you do more than reach the participants in that game. In most mediums, more individuals participate passively than participate actively. Two examples of this are YouTube and Wikipedia. The huge numbers of people who read or watch what has been published exceeds by far the number of people who contribute material. This means that, in addition to the actual participants in an ARG, there are also the *lurkers* – persons who have an interest, who read, watch and listen to the narrative as it unfolds but are not visible as active participants. What is important to remember here is that these individuals might be as interested in participating as active members, although they might not feel comfortable exposing their presence. But this does not mean that they are less important. So anticipate lurkers, and create rooms for lurkers to feel welcome.

The next audience, which is of equal importance, includes the *buzzers* and *mediaites*. These are persons who are not participating in the ARG but have an interest in the game that you are promoting or how the ARG is performing. Mostly you will find these in the press and media that cover the video game industry, both professional press and private persons with a high engagement in the industry. In short, these are persons who have impact on gamers and others. It is important to relate to these people because they have the possibility to further promote your games, by covering it in articles and other formats – although keeping the ARG design aesthetic of "this is not a game" will have to define how you engage buzzers and mediaites.

Alternate Reality Games, we believe, are of interest to the video game industry because the structure of promotion is similar to what the industry creates – games. The consumer should have a game state of mind when engaging with this product. In our experience with ARGs we have found that they seem incredible engaging. As The Beast closed down, consumers were left wanting more. But, as the point of ARGs is to not announce the game but to let the consumer find it, there are today communities dedicated to finding them. By our definition, these include consumers that who are highly engaged, consumers who want more, and consumers you want to communicate with as a game developer looking for the next Alternate Reality Game.

Exercises

1   How would you go about creating an ARG for your games?
2   Is it possible to create a game concept that uses the ARG and the platform for the game?

References

Ansoff, H. Igor (1957). Strategies for Diversification. *Harvard Business Review*, 35(2): 113–124.

Assael, Henry (1988). *Consumer, Behaviour and Marketing Action.* Boston: Kent.

Hirschman, Elizabeth C. (1983). Aesthetics, Ideologies and the Limits of the Marketing Concept. *Journal of Marketing*, 47(3): 45–55.

Kotler, Philip, Armstrong, Gary, Wong, Veronica, and Saunders, John (2008). *Principles of Marketing.* 5th European edition. Harlow: Prentice Hall.

Maslow, A. H. (1954). *Motivation and Personality.* New York: Harper & Row.

Oliver, Richard L. (1997). *Satisfaction: A Behavioral Perspective on the Consumer.* New York: McGraw-Hill.

Rogers, Everett (1995). *Diffusion of Innovations.* 4th edition. New York: Free Press.

Saussure, Ferdinand de (1916/1995). *Course in General Linguistics.* London: Gerald Duckworth.

Shostack, G. Lynn (1977). Breaking Free from Product Marketing. *Journal of Marketing*, 41(2): 73–80.

Zackariasson, Peter, and Wilson, Timothy L., eds. (2012). *The Video Game Industry: Formation, Present State and Future.* New York: Routledge.

Index